STEPHEN CLARK

CW01431579

AN UNNA2URAL WAX PRODUCT.

MADE IN LOCHEND, EDINBURGH, SCOTLAND.

2017.

2X

Unna2ural Wax

FRIED CHICKEN

17.11.2016

Jesus is serving tonight. I've eaten fried chicken for four days straight now and I'm feeling fine. There was an Eastern European guy working here last night and he seemed more managerial than Jesus, but he messed up my order and put ice in my drink. I definitely asked for no ice, but I put it down to him mishearing me - a Belfast accent is a hard one to shake off. Maybe he thought I said something about fries? Jesus is cool though. No matter how busy this little grease shack becomes, Jesus never misses a beat. So, tonight I've got my bucket of dead birds, some fries and a gas filled orange flavoured drink with no ice, and all is well with the world. In the distance I can hear a teenage girl exclaiming "Oh my God!", before Jesus smiles at me and says "Enjoy your meal".

I lift the little red plastic tray that my dinner is resting on, and I make my way to an empty booth in the darkest corner of the restaurant. The table is semi clean and therefore good enough for me to eat my dinner off, but not good enough for me to rest my elbows or phone on. Once I have offloaded my cargo, I squeeze my size 12 feet through the tiny stools that are bolted to the ground around the entrance to the booth, then swing my ass westerly and fall backwards onto the horseshoe shaped red sofa that runs around the inside. From my new vantage point I can gaze around the room at my fellow diners, most of whom are young couples. I decide that I'm not all that interested in what's going on around me any more, and for the next few minutes, as I shovel greasy mouthfuls of fried chicken into my face, I gaze into my cardboard bucket and think.

I moved back to Edinburgh two months ago. For six years prior to that I had been living further north, in and around Perth. Most of those years had had catastrophic moments in them, but the final two were a complete disaster. This Summer, as my little train bounced well off the tracks, I decided to just leave it there, derailed, and move on. The obvious place for me to go and rebuild my life was my home town of Belfast. I have lots of family there and it's the home of my favourite club night, Shine. They also understand that a pint of Guinness should be smooth and creamy, and not full of bubbles and served in a Tennent's glass. However, I opted to move to Edinburgh. I'd lived here for five years before I moved to Perthshire. I had run club nights here. I'd had a little dance, made a little love and generally got down all over town. Besides, apart from all of that tomfoolery and ballyhoo, my old boss had offered me a job. So, I packed my trunk and said goodbye to the circus.

The trouble is that everything hasn't exactly clicked into place. I'm paying more to live in a tiny attic bedroom in Edinburgh than I did to live in a two bedroom flat in Perth. I'm working shifts, which means I often see the broken undercarriage of the capital as I make my hour long walks across it's darkened streets to and from work. Lonely staggering drunks winding their way home, fast walking junkies with their hooded heads bowed, homeless people sleeping in department store doorways and greasy haired hookers trying to keep warm by dancing in small steps while they rub their cold hands together. Sometimes I hum Bernard Herrmann's score to Taxi Driver as I step over puddles and feel the rain dripping off the end of my nose. occasionally it feels like the darkness is gathering around me. There was an attempted murder in the park last night, just across the road from where I'm staying. I was walking past as the victim was being driven away in an ambulance with a police escort. "All the animals come out at night.".

I suddenly realise that there is nothing left in my cardboard bucket except a few tiny bones resting in a puddle of grease. I finish my ice free fizzy what-have-you in one go and then I start to clear up the mess I have made of myself. Jesus didn't give me enough paper towels to deal with this shit.

BEAUTIFUL BUNDORAN

15.11.2016

The insides of my eyelids are pink and burning. The morning sunlight must be flooding through those pale, thin, curtains again. Maybe it's the afternoon already? I wish someone would open a window, it smells like vomit in here. I need to piss. Maybe I can just drift off again if I try not to think about it? My head is thumping. It's actually making a thumping sound. I've never heard my head thump before, must be the tequila - I can still taste the salt, and I want to throw up. Thump, bang, thump, thump. It's getting louder. I can hear voices. I'm hearing actual voices. This is the worst hangover ever, today is going to be a nightmare and I want to be dead. Someone is shouting behind the door. I open my eyes and the light floods my brain and through it all I can see bodies. My fellow revellers are in various states of undress and unconsciousness, except for Johnny. Johnny is standing to the side of the door, he's fully dressed and he looks frightened. He gazes straight at me as he puts his left index finger across his lips to silence me. I nod my head in acknowledgement as I watch his right hand unlock the door, and in the same moment the door flies open and the handle cracks the wall. As Johnny darts into the bathroom and closes the door behind him, six men clutching hurley sticks enter the room. Suddenly everyone is awake.

Sometime in the mid 1990's I started going on Summer holiday's to Bundoran with my mates. We would each bring £100 or so (more as the years rolled on), most of which would be spent unwisely, and it was great fun. The first time we went there I was 14 years old. I rode the bus up from Belfast with seven friends, each armed with a sleeping bag and a few of bottles of (Ye) Olde English cider. We had a couple of tents between us, and I had brought along a twin cassette deck ghetto blaster, enough batteries to last the weekend, and a dozen or so Hardcore Rave tapes to entertain my fellow travellers with. The sound of the bass from my sound machine ensured that our little gang owned the entire back of the bus the whole way there, and it helped to set the tone for the trip. This was our holiday. No parents and no teachers, just Hardcore and cider. Oh, and girls - there'd better be some bloody girls there! As soon as we arrived there we fell straight out of the bus and through the doors of The Station Bar. I got the drinks in.

I'd been getting the drinks in for everyone for well over a year already as, at six foot and three inches in height, I towered above most of my friends. Every weekend throughout the Winter months I'd find myself stood in line outside a Belfast off license. The Troubles were still an ongoing situation, so you would need to wait outside to get buzzed through a heavy door. Once inside, I'd stand up tall, dressed in my black bomber jacket (a popular style in Belfast back then!), luminous yellow Rave t-shirt, snow combat trousers and heavy black boots. I'd feel my heart beating in my neck as I rehearsed my order in my head. The actual goods were kept behind a concrete wall, so you would have to bark your order through a little hole in some wrought iron before it was brought to you. Whoever was in front of me in the queue would suddenly disappear and then I'd step forward, look the server in the eyes and say; "Hi, I need five litre bottles of Olde English, twelve cans of Harp, a six pack of Miller, three bottles of Pink Lambrini (There were always a few girl's around), and a bottle of Ravers.".

We settled ourselves into The Station Bar in no time. By settling in I mean taking over the entire back end of the bar, including the pool table, and filling the jukebox with coins and, in turn, the room with the sound of Ultrasonic, "1, 1-2... Rezerection! U.S. back with the Hardcore!". My first drink was a large Bailey's with ice, which I enjoyed with a cigar - indoors! I was happy, my friends were happy and all was well with the world. However, the good times never last, and within hours of our arrival our tents had collapsed under torrential rain and we found ourselves huddled inside a strangers caravan sharing a wet bag of chips and some cigarettes that I'd swapped my ghetto blaster for. It was all for the greater good though, as I've never allowed myself to be that skint again.

In the following years we were much better prepared. We'd book family rooms over the phone at unsuspecting B&B's, then arrive like we'd just broken out of a borstal. We got to know the cool nightclubs, and some of them would even play my early productions - as long as the DJ received a free beer along with my home made CD. I used to like hearing my songs through the big speakers, watching groups of girls dancing to my beats or shouting "Tasteless twat!" to my mates if I spotted anyone leaving the floor. There was even one club there that had a vibrating floor, but most of these places just had sticky carpets and tequila slammers. Sometimes I'd get lucky and end up walking along the sea front in the pitch black, freezing cold, of the wee hours, holding hands with a local girl, or maybe one from Derry. I'd sit down on the wall outside the amusement arcade with my back to the broad Atlantic Ocean, then I'd take both of her hands and pull her towards me and we'd kiss. Big, long, soft, salty, teenage kisses with all eyes closed and nothing but the sound of distant waves as a distraction. I'm not much good at remembering names now, and I wasn't any good then either. I mean, a girl might shout "Hi, I'm Amy!" into my ear over the roar of a Jackson 5 remix in the back room of a nightclub, and I think, that's cool - Amy - got it. But, by the time I find out if it's Classic Coke or Diet Coke that she wants with her Smirnoff, Amy could be Annie - and saying Annie could mean the deal is off. So, I tend to stick with Beautiful or Gorgeous in an effort to keep my hat in the ring. Mobile phones are great though - "How do you spell your name?", "A-M-Y", "Oh, I thought it had two M's in it. Want another drink? Diet Coke, right?", "White Lemonade.". I always sat down on the wall to kiss because of my height. The downside to this is that I don't have much of an ass, and what I do have would be wet and frozen within seconds of impact with said wall. Thus ensuring that I wouldn't get any of that, sexy, girls hand in boys back pocket walk that was popular in the mid nineties. I called it the pick pocket - "You'll not find much in there love.".

"You've got one minute to get your stuff the fuck out of

here boys, or you're getting battered!" shouts the pudgy ringleader. The wee fucker looks like he means it too. His five buddies are all dressed in standard issue country boy clothing; checked shirts with around half of the buttons undone, blue jeans that have been lived in for a year and a half, and desert boots covered in cow shit. Four hours ago we'd have battered them senseless, but now that we're all drool, vomit breath and erections, physical violence is off the cards. Johnny re-enters the bedroom, grabs his already packed stuff and gets the fuck out of here, as requested. The rest of us get dressed quickly, throwing what we can into bags before we leg it out the door. No one wants to be last out, and it ain't gonna be me. I bounce over the next bed, knocking over cans and overflowing ashtrays as I go. "You wee..." - I'm gone. Along the shitty corridor, down the pishy stairs, past the receptionist - "Morning" - and into the light of daytime Bundoran. Pensioners are walking dogs and children are licking ice creams as my friend Bobby runs passed me, holding his jeans up around his waist with his left hand. Further down the main street we can see Johnny, he's waving us into an amusement arcade.

Minutes later we're in the back room of the arcade playing pool and Johnny is putting us straight; "Breakfast. We paid for breakfast, so I went down and drank all the orange juice.". "So?", says Bobby, realising that his jeans are on back to front. "Well, I drank all of the orange juice in the room. It was on all of the tables, in the middle of them in big jugs, and I was thirsty.". "You wee dick!", says, pretty much, everyone in unison. In the far corner two Bikers are playing on the glow in the dark air hockey table, while a third is putting money into the jukebox. "Killing In The Name" by Rage Against The Machine starts up; "Some of those that work forces, are the same that burn crosses.". My little gang of pals are in a sorry state, and the floor is moving slowly as our teenage stomachs churn. Everyone looks lost, like they want to be back home. Maybe we should all be taking school seriously? The music rises; "And now you do what they told ya. And now you do what they told ya...". Bobby starts laughing as he takes a seat to sort out his jeans. I look around the room and survey the scene, then I start laughing too. Johnny, shouting over the music, says "Anybody up for a pint?". Suddenly everyone is in stitches, and for a moment we seem to forget that we have hangovers. I rest my head back against the wooden wall. I can see cigarette smoke rising though the lights above the pool tables, then I close my burning eyes and it feels good. A sound like thunder begins to shake the floor; "Fuck you, I won't do what you tell me! Fuck you, I won't do what you tell me!".

SEXY DAISY

30.11.2016

"Daisy, Daisy, tell me how your garden grows,
because I want to know.
Daisy, Daisy, tell me how your garden grew,
because I love you.
Daisy, Daisy, how does it feel to be the
only girl in my life?

Daisy, Daisy, take me by the hand because
I want you to be my wife."

On a sunny, Saturday, afternoon, some time after the dawning of the millennium, I stepped out of a hot bubble bath in my one bedroom flat on a sink estate on the outskirts of Belfast, dried myself off with a towel that had the texture of heavy abrasive sandpaper, slipped on a pair of clean boxer shorts, and bounced across the hallway. Jamaican Dub music was playing low on a small, silver, machine that was resting on a plastic chair that I had painted navy blue and the carpet was covered in the hair that I had just shaved off my head. I landed in the kitchen. The room was coloured orange, apart from the cupboards which were all navy blue, and it was lit by a single, naked, bulb that hung from the ceiling in the centre of the room. Like all of the other rooms in the flat, the curtains were drawn, permanently. My mobile phone was resting on the work surface beside the kettle, and it was plugged into the wall. I picked up the phone and read the text message that was waiting there for me. Then I set the phone back down and made my way across the floor to another of my painted, plastic, chairs and sat down. As the chair began to freeze my arse off, I gazed at my set of cheap, navy blue, kitchen knives and thought about how I was going to kill myself.

I had been on the tear around the town with Johnny on the night that I met Daisy. We ended up at The Egg and, at 19, it was still a bit of a novelty not having to worry about I.D. to gain entry to this, student fuelled, vodka den. Johnny and I had been going to The Egg since we were 15, ever since he worked out how to make fake I.D.'s using his school's printer and laminate machine. Back then it was all about trying to make £20 last a whole night, and that included chipping in for a late night private taxi back to the badlands. There were no night buses to stumble onto, and walking home through the tribal patchwork of Belfast streets in the small hours could too easily have become the last thing you ever did. By the time we were 19 though, money was less of a problem. I was working at my Grandfather's photographic studio, and I was earning enough to ride a, nearly, new scooter and dress as sharply as any Mod in Quadrophenia. By day I'd be taking passport photograph's and showing young couples our "stunning range" of wedding albums, and by night I'd be cruising the streets of the city in my sandstone parka jacket and grey suede shoes, stopping every once in a while to take off my helmet, shake out my Beatles hair cut and blow cigarette smoke towards the stars.

That night, as Johnny and I walked up the stairs inside The Egg, the finest female ass that either of us had ever seen in our, relatively, short lives happened to be climbing the stairs just in front of us - approximately six inches from my face, as it happens. Some of my memories are vague but this one, dear reader, is not. This vision was squeezed inside dark blue hipster style jeans (it was the 1990's), and these dark blue jeans, in turn, had a kind of silver, tattooed effect, stitching, which further highlighted the ass in question - and, like I said, all of this was happening about six inches away from my stupid, wannabe Mod, face. After exchanging wide eyed glances at each other, Johnny and I decided that the best thing to do was to get drunk, listening to "Blue (Da Ba Dee)" and "Firestarter", and forget about it. I mean, this girl was beautiful. Long blonde hair, pearly white smile, body to kill for - your general nightmare really; made you feel ugly as fuck on sight. Best to not make eye contact. Just go and find a toothless simpleton to stand beside and wait for the shit to die down.

A few hours later and Johnny and I were outside in the street, covered in burger grease and hunting for a taxi. Well, I was hunting for a taxi while Johnny was embarrassing me by asking for the phone number of anyone vaguely female looking who happened to be near him. The Egg is situated in the heart of student land, and it was kicking out time at all of the nearby pubs and clubs as well, this meant that our chances of getting a taxi anytime soon were slim. So, I soon found myself leaning against a wall next to a cash machine, fumbling through the contents of my jacket pockets in search of a cigarette and a clipper. I could hear Johnny trying his luck with the girls who we're using the cash machine, and his patter was getting me down. I looked towards the ground and said "Shut the fuck up mate. Leave the girls alone and come and have a smoke.". I produced my flammable material and I sparked up. I could hear the girl beside me say "I have no interest in you, but I think your friend is hot.". I turned my head slowly to the left, following the dark lines that were etched into the pavement. I could see painted toenails inside thinly strapped, silver, high heels. They were coming out from under a pair of standard issue, 1999, flared jeans. My eyes followed the seam along the side of the leg, silver stitching - THEE silver stitching! I dropped my stinking cigarette to my right hand side as I turned, slowly, to my left. There, lying backwards, bathing in the light of the cash machine, was the vision. Suddenly, the vision's, big, blue eyes were looking right into my, 19 year old, hazel green eyes, and I was gazing back at her beautiful wet lips as they parted and she said, "Hi, I'm Daisy.".

As clear as my memory is of the first night I met Daisy,

the four years that followed are a bit of a steamy, hot, blur. I know that we had sex, LOTS of sex. I mean, I'm sure that we stopped every now and then to eat and drink and stuff, I just don't remember it. I can remember that her bedroom was in the attic of a large student flat that was owned by her father, and that she loved literature. She had a poster on one of the wall's in her room, it had photograph's of nine famous Irish authors on it, along with quotes attributed to them. I probably knew them all off by heart at the time, as I used to gaze at it in the mornings when Daisy went to university and I kept my uneducated head on her pillow waiting for her to return and kiss me all over again. The Samuel Beckett quote was my favourite, it was the final line from Krapp's Last Tape. Somehow, in amongst the endless sex scenes, Daisy managed to get a degree. I went along to watch her graduate, and as I sat beside her parents, waiting for the show to start, a group of twenty or so people arrived through a door at the far side of the room. "They all got the same bus.", I said to her Dad, and he thought it was really funny, and looked at me like I was Dave Allen. I was going to make a great son in law.

Soon after Daisy's graduation, I picked up my phone and I read the text message that was waiting for me. Daisy was breaking up with me, and moving to Bradford to do something that I can no longer recall. In that moment my life seemed completely worthless, and I really didn't want to be alive any more. I did think about my family and friends and things like that, but that's not what persuaded me not to kill myself. In truth, I can't actually remember what did. Just as I can so clearly recall the exact moment that I met Daisy, but next to nothing about the four years that we spent together, I can vividly recall the exact moment that I decided to kill myself, but not the reason that I decided to stay alive. What I can remember doing is going to Waterstones book store in Belfast and buying a little pocket book about women and, through using my new found wisdom, winning Daisy back. It was never the same though, although I seem to remember even more sex this time around, the magnetic forces that had once brought us together now seemed to be pushing us apart. We'd both been through some heavy life experiences together by that point, and there were just too many obstacles between us, the biggest and most obvious one being the Irish Sea.

A few lifetimes later and I was in a pub in Edinburgh. It was Saint Patrick's Day, and I was out celebrating the event with my new, serious, girlfriend and some friends when, from nowhere, Daisy appeared by my side. It was nice to see her and she looked as gorgeous as ever, but we couldn't really get to talking. She was visiting Edinburgh with her new boyfriend from Bradford, and I was with my new girlfriend. There really wasn't much we could say to each other. So, we went with a quiet "Hi", followed by some small talk about promotional Guinness hats. Outside the pub, traffic was moving. The world was still spinning around a sun in a universe so large that it's really difficult to even grasp in your mind. Yet, there we were, close enough to touch, but not rousing.

BUDDY HOLLY

12.12.2016

It's a Monday night, mid-December 2016, and I'm typing these words into my laptop as I'm lying, on my front, on top of my rented bed in a little attic room in Edinburgh. I can hear a teenage boy shouting abuse at somebody, who seems to be just quietly taking it, in the street below. From the sound that this squealing little twat is making, I reckon he must be standing near the bus stop. I'm also aware that there is a plastic bag filled with dog shit swinging in the tree somewhere above where his horrible little head must be. I know this because it has become the main thing that draws my eye whenever I look out of the living room window. It has been there since Saturday, and I keep thinking about the person who threw it up into the tree. Did they go to the trouble of bagging up their own dog's shit before flinging it towards the sky, or was it pre-bagged and just lying around? There's a bin at the bus stop, so choosing to dispose of said bag in such a manner is quite a statement. Maybe they hate our tree owning neighbour? Perhaps there has been a dispute at his garden gate regarding the sudden increase in dog shit on the kerb outside his house? I hope so, as much as I hope that a sudden gust of wind, coupled with gravity doing it's thing, will conspire to cover this nasty, foul-mouthed, kid in three day old mutt crap. However, life rarely seems to work out just as I want it to.

I open a new window in my browser, as there's a song that I want to hear so that it can finally leave me alone. It is a song that has been in my head all day long, coupled with images from a long time ago. I press play and the rolling tape sound reminds me of an old Hi-Fi unit that stood in my parents front room. It had wooden panels along it's side, and silver machinery housed behind a glass door. I can see it's Lo-Fi stylus cutting it's way through the grooves of an old, worn out, vinyl record. A melody that seems to be coming from a vintage, wind up, music box begins to fill my flickering mind as I drift from the present into the past. I'm going to the place that this innocent little melody is taking me. Maybe it's not a music box. It sounds like someone playing milk bottles, and I can remember those too. They were delivered to my parents front door everyday except Sunday... "Everyday it's a-gettin' closer...". Most days the birds would get to the milk before I did. They would peck their way through the silver foil top that indicated to the world that we were a full fat family, then they would drink the cream that had found it's way to the top, leaving me with dirty milk to pour over my cereal... "Goin' faster than a roller coaster...". I had better luck on Saturdays though, as we got two bottles on a Saturday so that the milkman could have a day off on Sunday... "Love like yours will surely come my way...". So, most Saturdays I got the cream... "A-hey, a-hey hey.".

This is my first memory. I can't remember being born, but my Mother tells me that it was agony and that she couldn't face me for 24 hours - and still, to this day, I like being on my own. I can't remember my first home, a flat in the suburbs of Belfast, amongst a patchwork of streets that had played host to all kinds of riots, shootings and murders during the darkest days of The Troubles. These were the days that I was being born into, a world were my name was chosen so that it wouldn't be obvious which side of the divide I came from. I can't recall any of that though. What I do remember is this; I'm 3 years old, standing to the left hand side of a large, brown, settee in my parents living room. My hair is in a side shade, and it's wet. I'm wearing a jumper that is multi-coloured, but prominently navy and grey, and it has red reindeer on it, but they are subtle. I am also wearing navy corduroy trousers, which are tastefully covering my brown Y-front's which have a cream "Y" on them. These pants are the worst thing that I can ever remember wearing, and I once wore luminous Bermuda shorts for an entire Summer season - in public. I was probably wearing brown shoes, it was 1983. Behind me is one of two enormous windows which make up one whole side of our living room. In front of me, sharing a seat that matches the settee, sit my parents. My Father is wearing a white work shirt with a packet of cigarettes showing through his pocket. He has a handlebar moustache, stubble, and jet black hair in a side shade. He looks like a Mexican outlaw at a job interview. My Mother is hiding under a tree that is made out of blonde hair. She is wearing a pink house coat, and is endlessly waving a pink slipper back and forth with her right foot. My Mother speaks, "Stephen, would you like a little brother, or sister?". I turn my little boy's body to the right, and I gaze out of the window, across the garden, beyond the road and stare at the gate posts at Peggy Sue's house.

My first friend was a girl. She was a year older than me, and her parents had named her Peggy Sue. I guess they were Buddy Holly fans. Her Dad was a bookmaker, and he used to say things like "It's forgivable to be skint, unforgivable to look skint.". I was the first kid on the block to work out that Santa Claus was the fat bloke that lived in my house all year round. I told Peggy Sue my theory while we played with her Barbie and Ken dolls inside her garden shed. I can remember that she was wearing a red Summer dress, her long, blonde, hair was catching the September sunlight as it danced through the open doorway, and her big, blue, eyes quickly filled with Hollywood tears as she screamed "Mummy!". When Mummy arrived, Peggy Sue brought her up to speed; "Stephen said that Santa Claus doesn't exist!". Her Mother then bent forward and gave Peggy Sue a hug as she said "There, there. Of course he exists.", and as she did so she winked at me. In that moment my childhood died. I had taken my first step towards adulthood, and all of the horrors that it had in store for me.

Peggy Sue had an older sister with a strange name who listened to "Walk Like An Egyptian" by The Bangles, and got headaches from the gas that emitted from her study table light. She also had an older brother who lived in Liverpool, where the football team came from, and an old, black, dog that mainly slept. Along with playing Barbie, I sometimes had to play "Shop". This just involved selling things to each other until we got bored of it. Then we might make some "Rose Perfume", the recipe for which involved an empty 1.75 litre Coke bottle filled with tap water, that we then shoved rose petals into that we would steal from a neighbours garden. We would then try to sell the putrid product to our Mum's. Sometimes we would eat the juice that we squeezed from Honeysuckles. Sometimes we would hear machine gun fire and be told to "Duck down, and stay quiet!". I got to play boys games too sometimes, like "Cribby". This involved standing at either side of the street and throwing a football towards the opposite kerb stone. If the ball hit the kerb stone, bounced back, and you caught it you would get a point. You earned 3 points if you managed to do this over the roof of a passing car. There was also a bit where you had to stand in the middle of the road, but I can't remember why. Every now and then you would hear British Army helicopters overhead and the low rumble of approaching Saxon vehicles. This would soon be followed by the sound of every dog in the neighbourhood barking as an army foot patrol came into view and made it's way along our street. Peggy Sue and I would just keep playing. Sometimes the soldiers would be pricks and kick our ball into a garden, other times they'd say "Alright?" in a strange accent as they walked by. There were better sounds that made there way into our street though. The Lemonade Man would jingle jangle his way into our lives every Thursday and take away our empty bottles and replace them with shiny new ones with unopened seals - Brown Lemonade, White Lemonade, Cola, Orangeade, Pineapple, Cherry and my favourite, (drum roll...) Cream Soda. The best sound, however, belonged to Teddy Ice, the ice cream man. My childhood ears could hear his bells playing "Teddy Bears' Picnic" three streets away. That would, usually, give me enough time to run into the house and persuade my Mum to part with an old fifty pence piece, then get back out into the street in time to be the first in the queue at the place where he always stopped - just outside Peggy Sue's. It was proper ice cream, chocolate, strawberry or vanilla, dug out of a tub and scooped into a cone. The measuring jug where he kept his scooper was on the counter in full view, and the water inside looked like mud. You could also opt for a Screwball, which was served in a little, clear, plastic cone and had a round and red piece of bubble gum at the end which would be frozen solid and covered in strawberry syrup. He sold Golden Wonder crisps and ice lollies like Funny Feet, Dracula and Big Feast.

Peggy Sue was also the first girl that I ever kissed. Our Mum's had taken us for a holiday in my Grandfather's caravan in Downings, county Donegal. The caravan was brown and cream, it was 1987. It was late at night and it was raining outside. I could hear the raindrops constantly exploding against the metal roof of the caravan as I poked my head through the crack in the orange curtains. As I watched the water running down the outside of the window in front of the endless, black, forever, I could hear the adults laughing and talking beyond the huge curtains that divided the room that Peggy Sue and I were "Sleeping" in, from the kitchen, lavatory (bucket), and proper bedrooms, that were now no longer ours to play in. Peggy Sue was lying on the U-shaped sofa in the living room, inside a sleeping bag, and I soon joined her. We only took up part of the U-shape, as we made more of an L-shape so that our heads could be beside each other. As we whispered to each other in the dark, Peggy Sue came up with a plan. "Do you think we should kiss?", she said. Her nose was about 3 inches from mine, and her face was slightly amber. I think it must have been light from one of those electric fires, or maybe just some of the light from the kitchen making it's way through the dividing curtains. Anyway, her face was slightly amber, and I said "Okay", and we both edged forward, tilted our heads to the right and pressed our lips together. Afterwards, we whispered to each other for a couple of minutes, then Peggy Sue got out of her sleeping bag, walked across the living room, through the big curtains and vomited onto the floor in front of our Mum's. I stayed where I was, lay my head back, and hoped there were no earwigs on my pillow. I had a big smile on my face that, had the light been on, would have shown the gaps were some of my milk teeth had fallen out that Summer. I was happy and I was sleepy. I had kissed a girl.

My eyes ran back over the street from Peggy Sue's gate posts. Back over our front garden, and in through the enormous window, as I turned left towards my parents. I had made up my mind about having a little brother, or sister, and I was about to say the first thing that I would ever remember saying. It went exactly like this; "No.". - Sometime, not long after my first memory, my brother, Paul, was born.

Many years later, long after we kissed, but not too long after Peggy Sue had moved away from our street, we met up, in Belfast city centre, and went to the cinema. An old fifty pence piece would get you fuck all in this place, and I spent all of the money I had with me on a "Small", orange, Fanta that was served in a bucket. Peggy Sue's Dad drove a taxi now, and he picked us up after the film and drove us to their new home, which was a B&B that the family now ran. Peggy Sue wore make up now and smelt of perfume. She even had boobs. Her bedroom was covered in Take That posters, and most of her stories were about boys. I wasn't interested in Take That, or boys, and now that our Cribby playing days were behind us we didn't seem to have much in common. I may have been the one to work out the Santa Claus scam first, but Peggy Sue definitely became a teenager before I did. It would be another couple of years before I'd kiss another girl and, unfortunately, it wasn't Peggy Sue. Like I said, life rarely seems to work out just as I want it to.

BLACK DOG

09.01.2017

I live in a small room at the top of a large house in Edinburgh. I share the house with a psychiatrist called Elaine, an orthodontist named Estelle and Jodie, an old, black, dog. Considering my current mental state, I'm in exactly the right place. Elaine can empathise with my low mood, Estelle can recognise when my face is showing signs of inner pain and Jodie can hang out with me like an old, familiar, friend. This is the place where I start, and finish, my days. It's where I can shelter from storms, recharge my aching body, and find some time to think, dream and rebuild my life.

I left home when I was 17 years old. At that time I was living with my Dad and my younger brother, Paul, in a large bungalow that we had grown up in on the outskirts of Belfast. Our parents had split up about about 6 years prior to that, and Dad had struggled to cope. He drank cider, lots of cider, and either sat in silence watching the television, or ranted about his divorce. Sometimes, if he wanted a rise out of me, he'd tell me how all music was shit after Freddie Mercury died. It was boring and tedious to listen to, so if we weren't hanging out with our mates my brother would play video games in his bedroom while I would put my headphones on and play Happy Hardcore on the decks in mine.

Music was my main form of escape at that time. If I went to school, the first thing I would do when I got home was listen to "Strings Of The Strings Of Life" by Derrick May, "Quarter Pounder" by Dave Angel or "Der Klang Der Familie" by 3 Phase feat. Dr Motte. If I didn't go to school, which was quite a lot, I'd invite some of my DJ obsessed friends over and we'd spend the afternoon playing tunes and smoking cigarettes, surrounded by posters of Begbie from Trainspotting, Pamela Anderson from Baywatch, and Rave flyers from Rezerection, Shave Yer Tongue and, local night, Choice at the Art College.

My high school was a fine place to lower your sights on life. It was all male and falling apart. At least half of my lessons were taught in freezing Portakabins, and lunch breaks were spent walking to chip shops in the rain listening to morons rating local joyriders like they were Pop stars. The boredom would occasionally be relieved with a sudden outburst of mindless violence. During various altercations I survived being headbutted, and punched in both the ear and nose. Because of my height I got quite good at putting rivals in a head lock, where I would then take pleasure in swinging them around at my leisure while their raging little faces grew redder and redder. Hardly a high point in my life though, and I left the place with few good memories, and 4 grade C's, 4 grade D's and an F in my GCSE's. Many faired a lot worse than me though, and not just with exam results. I have a vivid memory of a boy being taken out of school assembly to be told that his Dad had been shot dead on his way to work. When another boy died on a school trip,

I decided that it would be a great place to leave.

My Dad was disappointed with my exam results and handed me the Yellow Pages to look for a college that would take me. I was disappointed with him slurring his words to a Chinese takeaway driver after midnight every night, then sleeping through his alarm in the morning and phoning his work to tell them that his car wouldn't start, again. So, I didn't really give a fuck about what he thought. Eventually, my Grandfather took me to The Black Man, or Belfast Metropolitan College as it was known to nobody, and I enrolled for A level courses in Media Studies, Geography and Sociology. I dropped out of college after the first year. I loved Media Studies, did well and never missed a class, but Geography was dull and Sociology, Jesus. I only took Sociology because I thought it was Psychology and it might be moderately interesting, it was neither. I also had to resit my Maths GCSE, which I achieved a D in, yet again.

Sometime during college I got involved in CB radio. I guess this was around 1998, so it's way before Facebook and dating apps, back when you had to talk to people before you slept with them. Anyway, I made a few friends on the airwaves, from both sides of the Peace Wall, and generally had a good time. I even ended up with a long term girlfriend from the other side of the tracks. In fact, she lived in a different city altogether and I would cycle 20-40 miles a week, deep into an area where a boy like me shouldn't have been if he didn't want to become a statistic, so we could make love, hug, kiss and sleep to the sounds of Maria Naylor and Everything But The Girl.

One night I came home to find that my Dad had taken my CB Radio and locked it in the boot of his car. I guess it was easier for him than actually talking to me. I had had girlfriends since I was 12, and first had sex when I had just turned 15. Handily, when I was 16, my Dad gave me a book titled "How To Talk To Your Child About Sex", before he ran out the door, jumped into a taxi and disappeared into the night. I don't think he really had a clue about my life, or the things that I was interested in, and didn't seem too bothered about researching them either. I would go out clubbing and come home after a great night dancing to the music that I loved, and he'd be giving it "Where were you to this time?", "I told you I was going to a Rave at Exit 15 with my mates.", "They're probably all on drugs, I suppose?", "Yeah, probably. I'm off to bed.". Without my CB Radio it would be back to using the land line phone in the hall to arrange dates and talk to my friends, and back to my Dad moaning about the phone bill. Then something in my head just clicked, and I realised that I didn't have to be there any more. So, I packed a bag, opened the window in my bedroom that the burglars used every time they stole my stuff, and I stepped out into a dark, mild, Summer night. Then I just started walking, and never looked back.

Around this time I bought the Manic Street Preachers album "This Is My Truth Tell Me Yours" in Smithfield Market, in the heart of Belfast. There's a song on that album that has kept drawing me back to it at various times over the years, it's called "Black Dog On My Shoulder". When I first heard it I didn't know that it was about depression, I just thought it was quite a sweet, comforting, song with some strange imagery. I've suffered with depression a few times now in my adult life, and it's rather tedious. This current bout has been the most severe, and it's been droning on for almost 2 years now. It's generally worse in the mornings, and I have these interweaving mantras that just don't stop. One says "I wish I was dead", and the other says "I hate my life". These thoughts spiral around my head, a head which feels like it's in a vice, for what feels like an eternity, but it's probably only 20 minutes, or so. I can't really cope well with new tasks either, as I get very stressed and that triggers a panic attack. I feel my chest compress like it's about to implode, while my head begins to issue a steady stream of cold sweat. At that moment I just want to be anywhere else on the planet, as long as it's far away from my shitty life. It is a living nightmare.

I've written about the first time my own black dog showed

up to lick my wounds when Daisy left me. After I decided not to kill myself I, rather unconsciously, began to kill off other things in my life, including the person I was and the people I knew at that time. Over a period of a year, or so, I went from being a clean shaven skin head, to being a long haired guy with a beard. The Mod clothing was ditched and I started dressing in black, from my leather jacket, through my t-shirt and jeans, to my boots. I changed my phone number and I stopped answering the door. I had been friends with Johnny for 6 or 7 years by then, but my brain told me that it had to end. He was the past, and I needed to have a future. I know that it's really messed up. I can remember diving at my television to turn it off if I heard the door knock, and knock, and knock. Standing in silence, in the dark, until I could hear his car drive away. That was a really strange time. I was still living on the sink estate on the outskirts of Belfast. I had my door kicked in by youths, the Police and the Fire Brigade. I drifted off to sleep to the sound of joyriders burning rubber, and woke to the sight of abandoned cars on fire in the street. I saw gangs with baseball bats and crowbars attacking each other, a screaming woman being dragged across the road, a drunk man with his dick in my letterbox at 3am screaming "Shirley!", and the second plane fly into the World Trade Center on live television.

Nine years later my black dog was by my side again, walking with me through the streets of Edinburgh. I was just about to turn 30, when suddenly my head felt like it was trapped under an elephant. I had planned to celebrate my birthday in Amsterdam with my family, and my girlfriends family, but I called it off. I was having trouble being in public. Cold sweats, fear, exhaustion. My only salvation was the music of J Dilla. I downloaded everything that he had produced and filled up my mp3 player, that got me to work and back every day. Zoning out of reality, and trying to learn the secrets of his strange grooves. I had lots of close friends at that time too, but I had to get away and leave my past behind me again. My girlfriend and I decided to move to the wilderness and live in a place that was so remote that it was a 7 mile round trip to put the bin out. There would be no leaving party, no phone signal and no internet. We bought a 16 year old car for £300, filled it with what we could and headed north into the coldest winter in living memory. But, that's another story.

Back in the here and now, and I have an actual black dog in my life. Jodie is a fine dog, and good company. She likes me, and I like her. I'm back in Edinburgh, and I have a lot to be thankful for. I have a job, and a home with live in healthcare professionals. Slowly, my creativity is returning, and I'm remembering the things that I like, the good stuff that makes me tick. The sadness, distress and general bewilderment that I feel are a natural by-product of what I've gone through in my personal life over the past couple of years. 6 months ago my life had completely collapsed and I found myself in my G.P.'s surgery with a resting heart rate of 157bpm at 8:50am. Since then I've slowly learned how to breathe again. I'll probably have to put up with the weird morning mantras for a while longer, but at least it's my voice. It could be worse, imagine if it was James Blunt and Adele, Christ. I guess I'm learning to live with the black dog.

DISK JOCKEY

25.01.2017

"As the eternal bore that was "The Naughties" shuffled off for good, the crew of the good ship Edinburgh Dream Factory downed a bottle of Sailor Jerry's rum and deleted their entire back catalogue! As the storm raged around them, the brave crew held tight to the freezing masts and threw the master tapes into the sea as they laughed manically, quoting lines from "Imagine" by John Lennon at each other."

(Nerdy Frames, New Zealand. 2010)

I'm currently enjoying a few days off work and it's great. I find It takes my body a couple of days to move down through the gears, until I'm moving slowly enough to take my eyes off the road for a minute and have a look around at what else I should be doing with my life. On New Years Day I listened to Brian Eno being interviewed by Jarvis Cocker on the radio and he said that in the coming year his resolution was to play more. So, I wrote "Play more" on a pink Post-it note and stuck it on my wardrobe door. Yesterday I wrote a song, my first in almost a year, and today I'm writing this and thinking about putting together a DJ mix to post online.

I think the world needs good DJ's now, perhaps, more than ever. There is more recorded music now than there was yesterday, and there'll be even more of it tomorrow. As consumers, we are drowning in digital. I suppose that this is true of all kinds of content, there's just too much of it. So, it's nice when you find a source that you can trust. Someone who has already sorted out the good from the not so good, so that you don't have to. For me, my sources tend to maybe be a little towards the edge. This means that huge parts of popular culture pass me by, but I'm OK with that. I'm more interested in things that people missed first time around, stuff that could now be re-evaluated. Or, better still, creations that had no interest in being found in the first place. I'm also drawn to people who have had success in the past, but who now do smaller projects that keep them busy. These folk tend to have a great overview of the cycles of art, life and death.

I've just had a quick look at my web bookmarks and a lot of the pages I visit are written by ideas people, the "What would happen if we turned it inside out?" types. Austin Kleon, David Byrne, John Cooper Clarke, Mike Skinner, Moby, Seth Godin and Bill Drummond are all there. Well, actually, they are not ALL there. Bill Drummond's website (http://www.penkilnburn.com/) is currently "Suspended until further notice", most likely due to the re-emergence of the Justified Ancients Of Mu Mu that is planned for the 23rd of August this year (2017) (See; http://k2planthireltd.com/). Thankfully, the website for his The 17 project is still functioning. I was a member of The 17, and the Score that I wrote back in 2008, titled "Dream", can be found here; http://www.the17.org/scores/338 . I've just read my Score again, for the first time in years, and I've decided to perform it again, hopefully tomorrow, at Waverley train station, here in Edinburgh. I think the Score is well written, and easy to follow. So, hopefully, it should be easy to play.

Finding my work with The 17 still available on the internet made me wonder if any of my other creations had survived my frequent culls. I have somewhere in the region of 50GB worth of my creative work gathering dust on hard drives and DVD's that I've carried with me through the years from home to home, and my Mum has back up copies of the lot back in Belfast. However, I tend to delete things pretty quickly from the internet, once I've deemed them to be no longer in line with how I'm currently feeling. So, I typed some of my long deleted aliases into Google and had a rummage. I quickly discovered that someone has started using the name Edinburgh Dream Factory, a Methodist church in fact. It seems good intentioned, and a worthy project "Combatting unemployment, homelessness, depression" and "Helping people's dreams come true". I can't argue with that, it all sounds good. However, back in 2007, when I used the name, my general idea was to start a club night in Edinburgh loosely based on Andy Warhol's Silver Factory. A place where someone could be a unicorn if they wanted to be a unicorn. A place where the music was good and the vibes were legendary. OK, it didn't combat homelessness, or any of that shit, but it made people's dreams come true. Well, OK, it made my dreams come true. Anyway, other than a few old listings on Sneaky Pete's website (That was the night club that the EDF nights were held at between 2007-9), and a few old blog posts from Nerdy Frames in New Zealand, I could only find a couple of videos. "Frame Fill Wrap by HASSELL, Condensed and Space Furniture" (https://www.youtube.com/watch?v=bNp--YxzYZI) features my song "Love Bubble". In 2010 Hassell were the largest architecture company in Australia and the 25th largest in the world, and I knew one of the girls in the video and she was involved in the project and liked my music. The other video, "Voxlogue feat. Mac Hertz - Dying Baby Dolphins - Edinburgh Dream Factory Remix" (https://www.youtube.com/watch?v=M88v_bER8Mc) was made right in the heart of my Edinburgh Dream Factory project.

In 2008 I decided to only work on remixes for other artists for a whole year. I remixed Plum, Hostage, Murray Bruce and a whole host of others that I can't remember. All of the remixes had a heavy sound. Maximalist, like Phil Spector reworking Hardcore Rave. The Plum track got played at a big closing party for some event in South Africa that I can't remember, and the Hostage track got played on Radio 1. This "Dying Baby Dolphins" track was all put together by different artists on MySpace. Ten years ago, at the time of writing, Myspace was where it was at if you were making music, and that's where I connected with a lot of the DJ's and artists that would go on to play at Edinburgh Dream Factory. The video was put together by Doctor Chop. While I was trying to be Tony Wilson, he was my Peter Saville. His videos were amazing mash ups that really made the atmosphere at EDF different to everything else that was going on in Edinburgh at that time. Those were the days of Blog House, which was colourful and fun. However, most of the other nights still had black screens with white lines waving about the place on them for hours. They looked like they'd all found their visuals in a skip after a Ritchie Hawtin gig. They bored me shitless. But, thanks to Doctor Chop, I had Jamie Lee Curtis working out on the walls (From "Perfect", 1985), or the video of "Bear Necessities" from the Jungle Book looping around the room to the sound of an Electro House bass line. We were having fun, and as we watched our nights fill up with smiling people dancing like Mowgli, we knew they were having fun too.

Fast forward to the here and now, and I've just finished a protest song sampling Donald Trump. It's called "American Carnage". The American DJ, Producer and protester Tommie Sunshine likes it. The strange thing is that it sounds like the remixes I was working on nearly a decade ago. This was entirely unintentional. When I started up my music making software I began by writing the bassline, and then I brought in some strings. Everything was nice and gentle. The sun was shining, maybe somewhere someone was falling in love. Then I made myself a coffee, had a quick look at Twitter and suddenly it's dark outside and I'm working with distortion and nuclear alarm type sounds. Hardcore Rave seems to run through my veins, and it feels like it has always been there. I remember watching Terminator 2 - Judgement Day when I was a kid, and really connecting to the idea that I was a robot inside. I knew that my surface area bled when I came off my bike or fell out of a tree, but I figured below that it would probably all be metal and I would live forever. I can remember sitting on a bench in primary school and having the synth hook from "Twilight Zone" by 2 Unlimited storming around inside my head. This was a huge moment for me, realising that I could hear music without having to listen to it - it was just there, floating around in my mind! The first 7" single I bought was "Wind It Up" by The Prodigy, and the first full length album I asked my Mum to buy me was "Behaviour" by The Pet Shop Boys (She bought it for me for Christmas on cassette). While other kids connected with middle aged men in blue jeans who played guitars, I was getting excited about electronic music.

By the time I was in high school DJ mix tapes were the new currency. Pablo Gargano and MC GQ at Hellraiser 4 (1993) (

https://www.youtube.com/watch?v=UHd0Z8gOhPY) was a classic. There were specialist local radio shows in Belfast like the BCR Club Dance Chart and A.W.O.L. too. As time moved on, DJ's like Tizer and Binman became popular, and I would make frequent trips into town to go clothes shopping in places like SNAFU in Church Lane, or buy some 12" vinyl at Underground Records on Queen Street. After I heard an advertisement on Eddie Wray's radio show, I convinced my Mum to take me to the Eclipse Disco Centre in East Belfast, and that's were I bought my first set of decks. 2x Soundlab belt drive turntables (with complimentary slipmats) and a Gemini mixer. I then bought a pair of Jamo D115 speakers, and with the £40 I had left I bought a tiny amplifier that was actually fantastic. It couldn't cope very well with my Hardcore records, and it gave them all a slight distortion and knocked the needles on my Uncles hand-me-down twin cassette deck into the red. This gave my mix tapes a driving sound with a heavier bass than my DJ friends could get on their set ups. I had an edge. It was through one of these friends that I got my first DJ gig.

Davey was obsessed with Tizer's mix tapes. He bought all of the same records that Tizer had, learned his scratch routines and could play his whole set live, beat perfect. I was a lot more interested in finding my own tunes, one's that nobody else had that were good. We used to go to each others houses instead of going to school, but we were still learning. He would talk me through spin-backs and quick cutting techniques, and I would explain to him that records had B-Side's and that finding his own sound was important. One sunny afternoon in 1996 Davey phoned me up to tell me that we had a gig that night, and I should make my way to his house after tea time. I wore my black hooded jumper which had a drawing of a stick man smoking a spliff on it, along with my black combat trousers and boots. Then I slipped my latest batch of Dutch, German and Belgian

Hardcore Rave records into my record bag and headed off to play my first DJ gig. What Davey hadn't told me was that the gig was a leaving party for Primary 7 pupils at a local school. To be fair, it was a decent set up. I guess the school must have paid for it. We were on an elevated stage with a decent sound system and a bank of disco lights, and the hall was packed with little kids raving to the heaviest underground sounds around. They seemed to be having a great time, unlike the various bewildered looking parents and teachers who were lining the walls. I suppose they thought we'd be playing things like The Monster Mash and The Time Warp, maybe some Jive Bunny And The Master Mixers. Sometime, towards the end of the gig, a small boy came on stage. He had jet black hair slicked back with product, he was wearing a shirt and tie and he had a request; could we play a slow song? Of course! Children need slow songs sometimes too, but we didn't have any. Davey riffled through his records and somehow struck gold. He produced a 7" of "Would I Lie To You?" by Charles and Eddie. It wasn't a slow song, but we told the kids that it was and they believed us. I mean, why wouldn't they? We were DJ's, with headphones, and everything. So, we ended the show by playing "Would I Lie To You?" by Charles and Eddie. The children held onto each other and danced in circles, the adults finally heard a song that they recognised and all was well with the world. When the record ended everybody clapped and a balding teacher gained a fleeting moment of popularity by saying that we could "Play one more number.". I was out of ideas, but Davey remembered that records had B-Side's. So, he flipped the record and played "Would I Lie To You? (Club Mix House)", and it seemed to unite the room. No longer bewildered, some of the parents and teachers even managed to move away from the walls, occasionally even nodding their heads in time with the beat. A group of rebel kids ran up the steps onto the stage and started to dance beside us. What did they care? This was their last day at this school anyway, they might as well have some fun. Amongst them all was the small boy with the tie, holding hands with a girl who was easily a foot taller than him. He'd been brave enough to ask us for a slow song in the middle of a Rave, and that had actually saved the gig. So, the site of him with this girl didn't surprise me at all. I wonder what he's up to now? I hope it's something fantastic.

Over the next few years I started to want to make my own records. So, I bought some synths and got on with doing that. I used to read The Rough Guide To Techno and try to imagine what the records were like that were described in that book. This was way before the internet made it possible to hear every available song with the luxury of just a few clicks. At that time there was just no way I was going to be able to hear most of these songs, but the writing was brilliant, and very inspiring. So, I made my own music to try and conjure up what I thought this music would sound like. Occasionally I'd come across a CD by an artist that was mentioned in The Rough Guide, like the time I found "A History Of Things To Come" by Ian O'Brien. That album has a lush track on it called "Vagalume" (

https://www.youtube.com/watch?v=IG0MdH46Vqc), and it just has this thing about it that removes me instantly from wherever I am and pulls me directly into the music.

For me, no other art form can so quickly transform the way I feel to such an extent that I almost become someone else, or forget entirely who I am, or where I am, than music. Yet, it slips away like something that was once just in the air. It's beautiful, and one of the most remarkable things that I've ever been fortunate enough to experience in this little ball of craziness that we've called life. If I ever make something as good as "Vegalume", my work here is done.

When I first moved to Edinburgh I started DJing at house parties. These were pretty wild affairs, and some of them went on for days. They were a great way to learn how to read a crowd though, and how to play for an audience. The key thing for me was to play some attention grabbing stuff at the start of my set. Most of the other DJ's at house parties played House music, and rarely moved off a set tempo. So, I'd start my set with some Hip Hop, maybe even spin in some remixes of Indie bands if they were cool enough and start to build up a party vibe. Then I could get into Techno, or Minimal, or whatever I fancied. I had more freedom to experiment that way, and people went with it. Pretty quickly I started to get invited to play at more house parties, and then I began to get asked to DJ in venues. The first of these events was at a small club, under a restaurant, in the city centre. I'd been asked to DJ at a birthday party for a girl I'd met at a party, so I asked my friend Scott if he'd be up for DJing alongside me and he was. The gig started at around 5:30pm on a Saturday, and we needed to be out of the room by 9pm, that's when the official, paid, DJ would take over. I presume the venue thought we'd be eating cake and playing party games, but the whole thing blew up pretty fast. Because it was downstairs, it felt like it was night time. We had quite a lot of friends show up, and because there was no one on the door a lot of random people just wandered in. The room was dark and filled with people. By 8pm bouncers had been drafted in, along with extra bar staff. I just stayed in the DJ booth, it felt safe in there. At 9pm the official DJ showed up and told us that he was under orders to calm the place down and thin out the crowd. Scott and I thought we were going to end up on some kind of black list. But, a few days later, I bumped into the restaurant-come-Rave boss and he told me that he'd had his highest ever takings that night. He never asked us back though, and he kept his money to himself.

Around this time I received an email from Bill Drummond that helped to draw my creative mind into focus. He said that at 27 I would have an overview of what had gone before and a vision of what was to come, and that I should quit rebelling and get on with doing something that I thought was worth doing. That night I set up a MySpace profile called Edinburgh Dream Factory, uploaded a photograph of a sundial, and started making new friends. Pretty quickly my project was being written about by music blogs from around the world and I was meeting childhood idols like Jez from Utah Saints. My new friends were booking artists for their clubs that were signed to the mighty Warp Records. They were winning music awards, or being asked to record their own Essential Mix for Radio 1. Things were happening, and I just got on with things by walking into situations and thinking, "What would Tony Wilson do?".

The first real club night that I played was at Red, a club in the Cowgate that went on to become Sneaky Pete's. I'd been to Red a few times before I moved to Edinburgh, and always thought I'd love to play it. It was small, dark and always had a crowd that was up for it. The night I was booked for was a Monday night. There were 3 DJ's on the bill, and the crowd looked like they'd been out partying since Thursday. I was on second, and the DJ before me was really good. Very smooth, dropping Laurent Garnier tracks, building the atmosphere. I was wearing a yellow t-shirt that had a vision board on it featuring lots of little pictures of things that I'd like to happen in my life. I also had a CD wallet filled with my favourite tunes and my Sennheiser headphones with me. "This is my last record.", said the smiling first DJ, as he unplugged his headphones and gave me some room to get set up. I'm not sure what I thought when I looked out at the room, and the room looked back at me. I'm not sure I had time to think, really. I just got on with the job at hand, and I got into the zone pretty quickly. I know I played Soul Of Man - "Dirty Waltzer" early on, and that was met with the approval of the parting DJ. After that it's all a bit of a blur, but I spun a few early Network Records cuts, an Altern-8 medley that I'd put together, and harder stuff by Surgeon and The Avent. The party people danced, whooped and whistled, and pretty soon my time was up. What happened next was unfortunate, but not for me. I turned to the next DJ and said "This is my last record.", smiled as I unplugged my headphones and gave him some room to get set up. Then he cross-faded the room into silence, and it stayed silent for a long time. The dance floor emptied. I tried to help, but he seemed busy. So, I left the stage and headed for the exit. As I passed the bar a small group of strangers stopped me, and one of the guys said "You were great man. You should go on again.". I thanked him, but headed home - I had to catch a flight the next morning. That flight took me to Belfast, where I DJ'd at Belfast Music Club. One of their previous guests had been David Holmes, but on that night it was just big old me. I managed to attract a crowd of family members, people who had previously been watching a match in the bar, the guy that ran the night, his girlfriend and some bar staff. Seeing that it was a special occasion, I had dressed up in a cape that had a luminous portrait of Elvis Presley on it, and he was wearing lipstick. It wasn't a complete disaster though. The guy who ran the night seemed to like the tunes, stuff by Depeche mode and Orbital, and 20 minutes from closing time a bunch of drunk girls arrived and managed to get everyone dancing. I'm not sure why I wore a cape. I later played at a Rave called Clutter House dressed like a deep sea fisherman, while I threw daffodils into the air. Some questions are best left unanswered. More famously, I took to wearing a mask. Lots of artists do this, and there are plenty of them now in the world of electronic music (http://ozedm.com/why-djs-wear-masks/761/). I guess the mask served a couple of purposes; It provided me with a little wall separating me from reality, and it gave my audience something slightly more interesting to look at than another dude with a beard, wearing a t-shirt and playing records.

The Red Star gig led to me getting my own club night, Edinburgh Dream Factory, which ran every couple of months for a couple of years (2007-09). There were some great parties, and a lot of talented people played there. I tried to have a gig element to the night, early on. So, I had Plum play, or I teamed up with STFU festival and had live electronic acts. The first ever EDF had Andy Glitch playing his first live set. I can remember playing "Thousand" by Moby that night, and the place was going crazy. After the show I was having drinks with the crew, and a kid, this young, wide eyed, man, pulled up the shutters to the club, ran inside, grabbed me by my arm and said "What is this called? This is all of the music that I Love!". It was nice to be making money while I was doing something that I loved as well. I can remember riding a rickshaw home with my brother, carrying flight cases filled with gear, while my pockets were stuffed with cash. The final EDF was an Edinburgh Festival special, in late August, with a 5am licence. There were people there from all over the world. Gary King and Beefy played across 4 decks and the place was rocking. I performed an hour long set, playing tracks like "Flying Fingers" by

Motorbass, keeping the pulse. Then, for some reason, I decided to play "Vagalume" by Ian O'Brien. As usual, I was lost in the music within seconds. I was wearing my mask and white gloves, and I can remember looking through my CD's thinking about what the hell I should play next. I mean, "Vagalume" is lovely and all, but it's a record with no beats and no bass line and this was a Rave. Then I just stopped searching and I raised my hands and looked at the ceiling. While I did this I could hear people shouting, screaming and whistling. I lowered my head and looked into the crowd and I could see people of all ages, races and sexual orientations completely lost in the music. At the front of the crowd, two of the cutest oriental girls I have ever seen were holding hands, and those hands were raised to the sky. Perhaps that strange, but glorious, moment when I unified a small gathering of people under the spell of a strange little song with no beats was my finest moment? After that, I decided to play "Lightworks" by J Dilla as my final record. The night ended at 5am after a set of dark and heavy Dubstep had been delivered by Andy Glitch, the man who had also ended the first Edinburgh Dream

Factory. The circle had been completed. We had unleashed some dark magic, and it was time to seal the tomb.

The following month I moved north, to Butterstone, with my girlfriend. We rented a cottage on a large country estate beside Loch Ordie. The scenery was beautiful. Amber, red, brown, green and purple, beneath the blue and white. It felt so relaxing being far away from everyone and everything after being so involved with this life for so long. At the end of the month, September 29th, 2010 - my 30th birthday - I woke up early, gathered wood for the fire, then set off to climb over Riemore Hill to the shores of Loch Benachally. I was wearing a black suit and tie, with a white shirt, and black walking boots. In my right hand I carried a small, silver, flight case. There were deer and rabbits on the hill, and a buzzard in the sky. The sun was warm on my back. I was too warm, in fact. So, I slipped off my jacket and carried it across my left shoulder. When I got to the top of the hill I took a minute to compose myself and take in the view. Loch

Benachally is quite a sight on a sunny Autumn day. Other than the boat house on it's shore, you can't see another building between the water and the sky. That is unless you count the Laird's House, but that's really just a series of walls now. Nonetheless, that's where I was headed to on that particular day. I found my way down the hill, into the valley, and straight into the ruin in not much time at all. I lay my jacket over a wall beside a dead tree that looked like it had blown over centuries ago, then I set the flight case down on the trunk of the tree and I opened it. I then removed the contents of the flight case and placed it inside a discarded tractor tire. The tractor tire was also lying on it's side, but it probably hadn't been in that position for as long as the tree had. The tractor tire now contained a firelighter, some kindling, some firewood, a pair of white cotton gloves, a white masquerade mask with the letters "E.D.F." written on it and a pair of Sennheiser headphones. I put my jacket back on and removed a Henri Winterman cigar and a butane lighter from it's inside pocket. Then I kneeled down and set fire to the firelighter. I watched the fire slowly spread through the kindling and up through the wood before I stood up and lit my cigar. After that, I just walked away.

BLACK OUT

20.02.2017

Late this Saturday night I stepped through the haar in
search of The Pond bar. It looked like Sick Boy's
establishment in the film T2 Trainspotting, except this
place was busy. Kenny Breaks was standing outside the
door having a smoke, and it was good to see him. Ten
years ago Kenny had asked me to DJ at his Red Star
Institute night at Red, then Red became Sneaky Pete's
and that's where I hosted my club night for the next few
years. Kenny had organised this "Save The Pond" night
too, and it was buzzing. He pointed to a block of flat's
beyond the neighbouring scrap merchants yard and said
"That's Sick Boy's place in Trainspotting 2". Fitting, I
thought. We made our way inside and I got the beers in.
There were many familiar faces in the room. Guys who
I'd DJ'd with over the years, and a few local legends who
I'd seen spin as far back as 2003, when I used to visit

Edinburgh from Belfast to catch up with my brother Paul, who moved here a few years before I did. Throughout what was left of the night I was introduced to people as Edinburgh Dream Factory, to which most folk gave a knowing nod. My old friend Martin was there, and he said he recognised me by the back of my head. "Is that because I'm going bald?" I said. "No, it's yer ears" he laughed. After the bell had been rung and the bar had been cleared, Martin and I walked through the streets of Leith with 9 free cans of beer from the DJ booth, and two heads buzzing with ideas. We ended up back at my place listening to old Hardcore records until 4:30am. Good times.

I'm slowly beginning to feel that things are starting to fall into place. I'm much more at peace with who I am, and aware of the things that make me happy. I'm also making time to feed my creative side. This week alone I've penned lyrics for an up and coming UK Hip Hop collective, uploaded my first DJ mix in years to Mixcloud and now I'm writing this post. I still have the odd day were I'm feeling under pressure, or a bit lost. Overall though, I'm getting better. Possibly the only thing that I might want to keep an eye on is my alcohol intake. As, over the past couple of months, I've drunk so much on a couple of occasions that large parts of the previous night are completely erased from my memory. On one night I popped into an old man's bar for a pint on my way home from work, and ended up hanging out for hours with a multi-millionaire Dundee United fan, and a strange collection of hardened drinkers, many of whom were wearing kilts. Other nights I have simply lost the power of speech, or made strange bets about "lovely kettles", that everyone concerned remembers, except me. I voiced my concerns about my black outs to Elaine, my live in psychiatrist, and she said it wasn't anything to worry about really. She said that I had been through a really tough few years, but now I'm coming out the far side of that, reinventing myself and finding peace. I also told her about my first ever black out, and she thought it was very funny. So, now I'll wrap this up by telling you about it too.

The first thing I can remember was the smell, strange perfume. I opened my eyes and I was in an unfamiliar room. The room was painted beige, with white curtains which were open to expose a view of a concrete building (Rather oddly, it's the building that I now work in, eleven years later.). I was naked, and I was a bit frightened. I turned my body slowly to the left and noticed that there was a woman with red hair lying asleep beside me. I had no fucking idea who she was, and she was naked too. I turned my body back to it's starting position and I could see my clothes and trainers scattered along the floor. With lightning speed I calculated the quickest way to get dressed and get out of there, and then I put the plan into action. I sat up slowly, then stepped out of the bed and into my jeans, slipped my feet into my trainers and grabbed my t-shirt. Then I put my socks into my pocket and walked quickly and quietly out of the bedroom door which, thankfully, was already open. The red head didn't move. She might have been awake, she may have been dead - I simply don't know. Suddenly, I found myself in another room looking at four identical doors and beginning to panic. After what felt like 15 minutes I realised that one of the doors had a letter box in it. Within seconds I was gone. My route took me down a set of stairs and out onto a busy pedestrian street. I had no idea what city I was in. I turned left and I just kept walking as the Summer sunlight burned into my brain. Eventually, through a side street, I saw Edinburgh castle. After that I was fine. OK, maybe stumbling like a sock-free tramp through the streets of the capital en route to The Meadows wasn't fine, but I was on my way home. When I finally arrived back at my top floor bedsit in Marchmont the ceiling in the hallway was being held up by scaffolding. This made me nervous, like I was in some kind of alternate universe. I turned the key and entered my room. There was no scaffolding, thankfully, and everything felt like home. My desktop computer was sitting on top of it's desk and my synthesisers were resting in their racks. My bookshelves were filled with books about art and music, and my aloe vera plant, that an old friend who had moved back to Australia had given me, was on the windowsill taking in the sunlight. I closed the curtains, kicked off my trainers and, still wearing my jeans, got into my single bed. I switched my phone off, just in case any information about the previous night was going to come through. Right then, everything felt normal again. That night I could hook up with my friend Scott and drink some of that £2.88 red wine from Tesco's, talk about meeting Tim Minchin and try to figure out who the red head was. Until then I was going to sleep the sleep of kings. Eyes closed. Black out.

STUDIO TIME

26.03.2017

Last week I stood on top of Black Mountain in Belfast and looked down into the city that I grew up in. It's changed a lot from the place that I remember from my teenage years, and that's a good thing. When I walk through it's streets now they're buzzing, happy and vibrant. It's a place that feels youthful and plugged into the wider world. When I was younger, the only time that I experienced that atmosphere in my home town was at Shine, my favourite club night. Now it seems like someone has managed to bottle the positive vibes of Rave culture, and pour them daily into the minds of the city's residents. It's rather fabulous, really. From that great vantage point above Belfast I could see the Mourne Mountains, Belfast Lough, Samson and Goliath (The towering cranes in the Harland and Wolff shipyard), Belfast City Hospital and The Ashby Building in Stranmillis, near where my old flame Daisy used to live. I could also see the City Cemetery, where my late Grandfather is buried.

My Grandfather, Pat, died on the 2nd of April, 2000. Although I attended his funeral, I couldn't recall ever visiting his grave since. So, as I climbed back down the mountain with my Mum and my Stepdad, we decided we'd drop by. His grave was easy to find, and his headstone is very distinctive as it has a camera etched onto it. This is fitting, as he had spent most of his life looking at the world through a lens. I can remember him telling me that he used to develop his own photographs under his bedsheets when he was a kid, and how this passion had driven him to get a job at the Ashleigh Studios in Royal Avenue. As far as I can recall, he started his own studio by operating out of his Mother's front room. Terrins Studio went on to be a very well known business at the corner of the Springfield and Falls Road's. Along with that, for a time he was also a cameraman for UTV, and made holiday video's and advertisements as well. This led to me starring in an advert for Spar, appearing as a cheeky child who caused their goods and prices to fall. I think I got an Optimus Prime Transformer toy as payment for my roll, along with the kudos that came with everyone in my school seeing me on TV every night for months. This was back in 1984, when there were four TV channels and no internet. So, everyone, and their Granny, saw me on the telly.

I quite liked visiting his grave. I'm a fan of graveyards in general. When I first moved to rural Perthshire I spent my first lunch break from work wandering around Greyfriars Cemetery in Perth, taking in the sunshine. While I was there I was approached by a homeless man called Stephen who had just been released from jail. He was munching his way through a whole chicken that he had just found in a bin outside Tesco's, and telling me about the best day of his life, when he went to a party on a beach somewhere along the north coast. That night, after work, I travelled through some of the most beautiful Autumnal scenery I had ever seen in my life. Through Dunkeld and up into the hills at Butterstone. Past Dougie MacLean's house, the writer of "Caledonia", and onto the country estate beside Loch Ordie where I'd spend the coming year lighting log fires, walking in private woods and looking at my favourite animal, deer, in the garden. I think that day, more than any other, perfectly sums up the life of extreme contrasts that I've always had.

This St Patrick's Day, during my Belfast visit, I met up with Jerry who worked at my Grandfather's studio for many years. He told me that old Johnny, who used to call into the studio every day to do The Star crossword with my Granda, used to come up and sit at his grave. I thought that was pretty cool. I'm an atheist, so I didn't stand around praying at the grave, or anything like that, when I visited it. I just like confronting death. It's not something I've ever been afraid of. I once wrote a track called "Song In The Cloud". It's a death song, like "Leader Of The Pack" or "Johnny Remember Me". I think death might just be the most fascinating thing about life, as it's the part that raises all of the big questions. When I was at the graveside, I just liked taking that short period of time to acknowledge the shared past that I had had with my Grandfather, and think about some days that are long gone and fading, but nonetheless helped shape and sculpt a part of the person that I am today.

I first worked for my Grandfather when I was 14. His studio ran the Santa's Grotto at Belfast's biggest toy store, and I was tasked with selling tickets and handing out photo's. Little did I know then that I'd still be doing those same tasks for money 23 years later, yikes! That was the year that Bill Clinton visited Belfast. Once again I ended up on TV when Patrick Kielty visited Santa's Grotto to do a segment for Talkback. My Grandfather's studio was just around the corner from McErlean's bakery, where Bill Clinton met Gerry Adams. There are photographs and video of Clinton's limo passing the front of the studio, and my grandfather took a photo of the pair of them shaking hands outside the bakery. A couple of years later my Mum was on the front page of most newspapers, and page 3 in The Sun, voting yes to the Good Friday Agreement - in her wedding dress! She made the right choice.

Sometime after I left college my Grandfather gave me a job at his studio. I loved it. I used to ride my scooter into work, then help out with framing photographs, making up wedding albums, taking passport photos and moving camera gear about. The Spring Fry was just up the street. So, at lunchtimes I'd stink the place out with curry chips. They did Chinese or Indian style curry sauce, and the chips were lovely. Sometimes there'd be a crowd of street drinkers outside, and mostly they were good humoured. Old Johnny might wander in in the afternoon and have a chat with my Granda about The Sweetie Bottle, an old shebeen, or unlicensed bar. Sometimes they'd talk about the Belfast Blitz, when the Nazi's bombed the city and my Grandfather and his family moved to a house in Cushendall, up the Antrim coast, and to relative safety. Other times they'd talk about the burning of Bombay Street, and the start of The Troubles.

I used to like to go out in the car with Jerry. He always had good taste in music, and would play things I'd never heard of before. Bands like Lemon Jelly and Bran Van 3000. We'd drive up the Newtownards Road listening to "Little Britain" by Dreadzone, or cruise down the Westlink to the sound of "God Is A DJ" by Faithless. He told me that, when I was a kid, my Grandad went to a meeting at the big toy store clutching a briefcase that I had stuck an Ozzy Osbourne sticker on, and he still got the job. He was once pulled out of his car by a Loyalist mob and roughed up, they only let him go when they found his union card. However, my Granda used to wear a Rangers tie to go and photograph weddings in West Belfast because he liked the tie. He didn't give a fuck. Some people even used to call him Terence, mistaking the Terrins in "Terrins Studio" to be his first name, but I don't think he ever corrected them. The older I get, the less I care about these kinds of things too. Don't sweat the small stuff.

I feel privileged to have caught the tail end of a generation who had lived through the twentieth century in a city that saw more upheaval than most. I saw the last embers flicker and die, then I watched their smoke dance off into the air. There are still plenty of people about who remember names like Crazy Horse, Jimbo and Johnny Marley. The days before mobile phones, when the coins in your pocket were bigger and heavier and you could buy more things with them. I can try and grasp at those times, but they just float out of my hand and retreat into the distance. I love hearing those tales though. Like how my Great Grandfather grew up in the countryside, won the football pools and moved to Belfast and opened a bar, and how that bar was then bombed in the early days of The Troubles. Or, how, as a child, my Mother used to walk along alleyway's to knock on a strangers back door and buy a bottle of vodka for her Aunt. Getting into the cinema for the price of a jam jar, Mickey Marley's Roundabout, Romper Room, holidays in Donegal, The Singing Pub, drinking the water at Lough Salt, the disappearing beach at Downings. There were bad times too, and many hundreds of days were nothing much happened at all. It's no different really to the times we are living through now. Much of the stress, strain and worry that we go through in our day to day existence just now will be long forgotten by the time we come to look back on it all, while we stand at another graveside many years from now.

My studio days ended when a car crashed into me as I was driving my scooter home from work, along the top of the Springfield Road, towards the junction with the Whiterock Road. I can remember flying through the air over the top of the car, and towards the pavement at the far side of the road. I woke up just around the corner from where my Grandfather is now buried with a crowd of people gathered around me and the sound of an ambulance approaching. My scooter was a write off, and the front end of it was embedded in the rear wheel arch of the car that hit me. The ambulance drove me past my Grandfather's studio to The Royal Victoria Hospital, the place where I'd been born 19 years previously. I spent what remained of the millennium in a cast which ran the length of my torso, walking on crutches and attending sessions of hydrotherapy. A few months after that, on the 2nd of April, 2000, my Grandfather died.

We have come full circle folks. Here endeth the lesson.

WRITING LYRICS

27.04.2017

"The secret of a song writer is to take the things that are close to you and make them so that they can be

universal." - Dougie MacLean

I've been wanting to write this chapter for about a month, but I was holding out until I finished the lyrics to the second song that I wanted to include in it. Tonight, I finished the lyrics. So, here goes...

I first wrote lyrics when I was a teenager. I bought an acoustic guitar, learned a few chords, and wrote songs about tearaway teenagers, love, Summer holidays and even one about a fictional missing child. Then I bought my first synthesizer and had some success making instrumental electronic music. So, I focussed on that instead.

Recently, I was asked if I'd write some lyrics for a member of an up and coming UK Hip Hop act. I said "Yes", and managed to write a descent song in about an hour. This has lead me to write two more songs of my own, with a view to recording them.

I remember watching a music documentary years ago that had a bit where Noel Gallagher was talking about the fact that he writes songs on a guitar, and that's why they don't come out sounding like Jean-Michel Jarre. I've had a think, and I'm going to try and record some very simple, stripped down, minimalist, electronic backing tracks. Then I'll add my vocals. In my mind they'll sound like Springsteen making his "Nebraska" album in Ableton. In reality, they'll probably sound like Yazoo, with Alison Moyet's incredible voice replaced by my, well, more functional one.

I listened to a Brian Eno interview recently, and he said "Lyrics are really the last very hard problem in making music.". I liked that. He talked about the possibility of lyric generators, and of how it's already easy to generate music. I was aware of this, as my brother, Paul, and I have both had national radio airplay with songs consisting of ready made loops. Eno himself creates entire albums that have been self generated. He basically sets up the sounds, and the parameters inside which they'll function, and then just starts them rolling. Then he chooses the most interesting sections. It's really an editing process. I'm drawn to the idea of lyrics being seen as something more of a challenge. The last great hurdle to be overcome before Pop eats itself.

Mike Skinner A.K.A. The Streets, is one of my favourite song writers. In his book, "The Story Of The Streets", he writes about listening to country songs and reading books on how to write songs by Sheila Davis. Mike has written some great tunes. My favourite is "On The Edge Of A Cliff", but "Dry Your Eyes", "Never Went To Church" and "Could Well Be In" are also fantastic. After reading his book, I bought all of the Sheila Davis books, and any other books on song writing I could find. A favourite being "The Songwriter's Handbook" by Tom T. Hall. I loved finding out about killer opening lines and power positions. This even lead to me reading Stephen Fry's "The Ode Less Travelled", then writing a poem a day for a month. When I was in my late teens I found that, a lot of the time, lyrics would ruin a good song for me. I was more into the rhythm, melody and feel of a song. So, having someone singing a load of lines that seemed to mean very little over the top of a good tune would just put me off the whole song. "Original Pirate Material", the first album by The Streets, is probably where my perception of the power of lyrics began to change.

I had always liked classic songs though. Powerful vocal performances, like Harry Nilsson singing "Without You", stick in the mind. Or, great lines like "I ain't got no cigarettes." from "King Of The Road" by Roger Miller. I was fortunate enough to live in the same Perthshire village as Dougie MacLean, Butterstone, during the worst Winter in living memory, 2010. His most famous song is "Caledonia", a love song to a country. It has a fantastic chorus, although I'm not sure if the verses would get past Sheila Davis without a bit of restructuring. "Solid Ground" is my favourite of his songs, and he keeps bees that make nice honey, I've had it on my toast. He also shares the same view as me on Scottish Independence - that it should happen. To my eternal regret, I didn't vote in the

2014 referendum. Although I had lived in Scotland for nine years by then, and paid my taxes, I didn't feel it was right for me to have a say. As the campaign's reached their conclusions it wasn't so much the positivity of the Yes camp that won me over, but the endless negativity from the No camp that pushed me away. By the time I was livid enough to take a stand, it was too late for me to register to vote. Since then, I like that Nicola Sturgeon has said "As far as I'm concerned, if you want to be Scottish you can be.".

I'm going to wrap up this chapter by presenting two new songs. I'm going through a divorce just now, so I thought it would be a good time to write a couple of break up songs. The first song is called "Waking Up Is The Worst Part Of Breaking Up.". I've had that line rattling around in my head since the Summer of last year, a time when my life was crumbling around my ears. It's a strong line, one that I think most people could connect with. I found it easy to write the rest of the song around that, as I tried to recall how I felt a year ago. The second song is called

"Our Union Is Over.". It's another break up song, but the twist this time is that it's actually about the end of the United Kingdom. A divorce song for our nations. Maybe there was something in that MacLean honey that got into my bloodstream?

OK, here goes something...

Waking Up Is The Worst Part Of Breaking Up
By Stephen Michael Clarke
27/02/2017

Here I'm lying in bed
Alone on the side where you slept
Thinking the day we wed
Those promises you never kept

I don't want to get up
Wish I could just go back to sleep
Maybe we could make up?
Even though you've hurt me so deep

Waking up is the worst part of breaking up

I never want to rise up in the dawn

Open my eyes then realise that you're gone

Waking up is the worst part of breaking up

How I wish we could go back to the start

You'd still be here instead of breaking my heart

I should have held your hand

Walking to our favourite place

Smiled at your wedding band

Felt you in a warming embrace

Watched osprey in the sky

Flying high through the Summer breeze

Now I just wonder why?

"I do" is not a guarantee

Waking up is the worst part of breaking up

I never want to rise up in the dawn

Open my eyes then realise that you're gone

Waking up is the worst part of breaking up

How I wish we could go back to the start

You'd still be here instead of breaking my heart

Waking up is the worst part of breaking up

I never want to rise up in the dawn

Open my eyes then realise that you're gone

Waking up is the worst part of breaking up

How I wish we could go back to the start

You'd still be here instead of breaking my heart

Our Union Is Over

By Stephen Michael Clarke

26/04/2017

Now is the time for us to part

Divorce and go our separate ways

So numb it might not break our hearts

We dream of freedom more each day

Our new hope is independence

We don't have all the answers yet

Now we're standing at the entrance

About to take our first brave step

Our union is over

Yet we will always be near

Standing shoulder to shoulder

Great memories to hold dear

Our union is over

We turn to face the world again

Bring our friends a bit closer

Sharing smiles we can't contain

Fear builds walls that one day crumble

They cannot hold the tide of hope

As we wait for them to tumble

For real change everyone must vote

Our new hope is independence

We don't have all the answers yet

Now we're standing at the entrance

About to take our first brave step

Our union is over

Yet we will always be near

Standing shoulder to shoulder

Great memories to hold dear

Our union is over

We turn to face the world again

Bring our friends a bit closer

Sharing smiles we can't contain

Our union is over

Yet we will always be near

Standing shoulder to shoulder

Great memories to hold dear

Our union is over

We turn to face the world again

Bring our friends a bit closer

Sharing smiles we can't contain

SHARP PAINS

31.05.2017

I'm writing this in the final hours of the last day of May, 2017. I'm lying outstretched on my front, on top of my bed, typing on my laptop. It's a warm night so I have my window open, and I'm down to just my boxer shorts so that I can feel the breeze on my skin. The scene is a far cry from anything remotely sexy, or stylish though. OK, I'm operating in low light, and there's a stack of books on my bedside and posters on my wall that would indicate that I have an interest in art, music and poetry. There are clothes in my wardrobe that may even indicate that I have style, and if you spent a few minutes rummaging through my belongings you'd no doubt discover that I'm sexual being. Not tonight though, I'm wreaked.

I need a holiday, and in fact I was due one, but work have put it back by three weeks. So, now I'm operating mainly in a kind of burnt out, zombie like mode. My days just seem to drift into each other without me having to be very much awake to get through them. If I'm being really honest, and I am, most of my life over the past few years has felt like that. I just don't really care too much about anything. Ten years ago I fully believed that I had the power within me to change a city. It didn't seem like a daft, or far fetched idea to make statements like that, or hang around with other folk who had big ideas. In retrospect, although it was exciting, I think it was probably an exhausting and ultimately disappointing way of existing. These days I process ideas in a much quieter and personal way. I still share my thoughts and the things that I create, but I don't really care if other people get the joke or not. I'm much more accepting that everyone else is on their own journey.

This stack of books by the bed thing, it's new. Well, it's new to me. Prior to this year I was a one book at a time kind of guy, and I always stuck with a book, even if it was shite, right through to it's bitter end. I could easily read a good book in one sitting though. Moby's memoir, "Porcelain", was the last book I did that with. Right now though, I've got a stack of 17 books by my bed, all active. In fairness, some are merely reference books. Books of lyrics by Lou Reed, Jarvis Cocker, Billy Bragg, Van Morrison and Chris Difford. Poetry books by John Cooper Clarke and Hollie McNish. "I Remember" by Joe Brainard, "45" by Bill Drummond. There's an anthology of early Irish lyrics that I picked up at No Alibis the last time I was in Belfast, and a book from the Bridget Riley exhibition I went to here in Edinburgh last month. There is a copy of the "New Illustrated Rock Handbook" from 1992. I got that book for Christmas when I was a kid, and I remember wanting to be one of the artists in the Appendix section at the back of the book. I never had any interest at all in being in a successful band, and I have never played air guitar, or sung into a hairbrush before thanking my imaginary stadium full of adoring fans. Perhaps I'm missing out, but I doubt it. Anyway, the Appendix section of this particular book is an A-Z of all of the artists who didn't quite make the grade, didn't quite do enough for music, to feature in the main part of the book alongside, ahem, great artists, like Michael Bolton and New Kids On The Block. I'll give you an example;

KING CURTIS - Wonderful R&B tenor sax player who fronted own band, as well as playing for Buddy Holly, Coasters, Donny Hathaway, and Aretha Franklin. 1971 classic album Live At The Filmore West proved testament to career that was cut tragically short when he was stabbed to death in New York the same year.

Now, at the time, I had no idea who King Curtis was, and no internet to find and play me his music within seconds. But, I did know that he sounded real, that his life story read like a movie plot, and that that single paragraph of information seemed way cooler than the seven paragraphs, discography, US and UK chart positions and full colour photograph that Terence Trent D'Arby had been afforded in the same book. I now know who King Curtis was and what he sounded like, and if you've ever watched the film "Withnail & I" then so do you. It's Curtis' live version of "A Whiter Shade Of Pale" that plays over the opening credits of the film. 25 years on and I still want to be in the Appendix, rather than the main body of

"The New Illustrated Rock Handbook". Perhaps, if I were ever judged to have style, I could trace it's origins back to making that choice as an 11 year old.

The remaining books in my pile are "The Rough Guide To The Best Music You've Never Heard", "Pop Grenade" by Matthew Collin, "The People's Songs" by Stuart Maconie, "Reelin' In The Years" by Mark Radcliffe and the "Main book, that I'm actually reading", if anyone asks; "A Year With Swollen Appendices" by Brian Eno. I also have many shelves laden with books on similar subjects, waiting to be read.

I've had to move around quite a lot over the past few years, and the toughest decisions I've had to make when I'm packing up are what books I'll leave behind. I've discarded books that are worth hundreds of pounds by Bill Drummond, along with books on some of my favourite producers, like Joe Meek, which are now long out of print. I could go on, but I'd rather not. Other than books, I'm about as minimalist as can be. I have some clothes, recently mainly black ones. I've noticed that Mike Skinner mainly wears black clothes, even shit from Asda, and it all looks cool as fuck. Black is timeless as well. For me, it's no logos and no writing. Everything plain. Black, white, navy or grey - that's it. I have a Harrington jacket that has a tartan trim, but that's acceptable provided it's worn with a plain white T-shirt and either my black jeans and black shoes, or grey jeans and jet black trainers. I've got suits, and shirts and oversized hoodies and all kinds of things actually. I'm quite happy with what I've got going on now, style wise, and I think it works for me. I became a much sharper dresser the first time my wife left me, and it's kind of stayed with me (At least something did - boom, boom.).

Other than my books and clothes, I've got this laptop that I'm typing on, and that I make music on. I've got a couple of synthesizers that I've had from back in the days when I made tracks that were relevant to other people. I've also got a camera. It's not an overly expensive one, but other than my laptop, it's the only, relatively, expensive thing that I've ever bought myself (and I got it on sale, and with double staff discount if I remember correctly (and I do)). That's about it really, the Clarke empire will be easy to divvy up once I've breathed my last. I quite like the fact that I could just walk out the door at any time, and just keep on walking. I could leave my little pile of things behind and not feel anything. Anyway, like I said, I'm in a not feeling frame of mind.

I've just had a look out of my window. I quite doing that because I can see lots of things, but no one can really see me. The main thing that catches my eye tonight is the Tardis across the street. It's a proper Doctor Who one, navy blue. I live in Edinburgh, and there are lots of Tardis' here (is the plural Tardi? - I can't be arsed Googling. Answers on a postcard to 10 Downing Street, London, Engerland) and many of them have been converted into little coffee shops and vegan what-have-you's, but there's not much call for that kind of thing all year 'round where I live. So, I have a proper Tardis to look at whenever I fancy. When I'd finished Tardis gazing I had a look around my little room. The floor is a sea of midweek carnage. Work shoes, an empty carton of Ben & Jerry's Core something-or-other, the remains of a fish supper, an empty glass bottle of Barr Lemonade and half a glass bottle of Irn Bru. There are little piles of coins and scribbled notes all over the show. Whisky bottles, cigars, paintings, ideas for songs, half finished lyrics, it's chaos really. This is all new, and it's all good. For years I've been trying to create things in neat little lines, trying to make order out of things. I'm older now though, and wise enough to know that nothing works out, really. Embracing the chaos, and making room for the happy accidents is where it's at.

I recorded three songs recently and they're all shit. That's OK though, most of the songs in the world are shit. Even great songwriters haven't got a great strike rate if you consider how many songs they write in their careers compared to how many hits they've had. It just takes one or two great songs to change a life though. A Christmas lyric that becomes a hit song would be the obvious jackpot, but since I can't stand Christmas, it would also be a kind of personal Hell. Perhaps some sort of Mungo Jerry "In The Summertime" thing would be better. Sell some sun protection, or ice cream with it. Fuck it, they could slap it onto whatever they wanted, as long as the cheques kept coming in. "Lamb face kebabs you say? Sure, no problem.". (At this point, I must be clear that I'd be the songwriter, ie. the guy profiting from the song, and the artist can be out there doing the heavy lifting. Think Hugh Grant's character in "About A Boy". Remember him? He lived in a nice apartment, no ties, no strings, hefty wallet, light mind, and all because his old man wrote a Christmas song. He was a bit of a prick really? Yeah, him. Well, that's me if my life pan's out. Anyway, I digress...).

So, I want to write more lyrics, and write more poems. I want to take more photographs, and make a short film, and go hill walking, and write more shit like this, and, and... The ideas are endless at the minute, and they're varied. The execution of these ideas is rarely all that it could be though. On Sunday I made a 30 minute Hardcore Rave DJ mix, as a homage to the lost world of the A Side's of C-60 cassette mixes. Who the fuck wants to listen to that? I did. Perhaps that's the best thing that I've got going for me at the minute. I don't really own anything, I'm living in a shoe box and I've got sharp pains between my shoulder blades that make me wish I was fucking dead. But, I don't really have anyone to answer to, and my general daily amount of fucks given remains at a slow and steady zero. It's something I can rely on. I've got my cornerstone, let the building commence.

REMOVAL MAN

23.06.2017

It's Friday afternoon. I finished work at 8pm on Saturday and I've been off since then on holiday. By 10pm Saturday night I was about 140th in a queue outside

Studio 24, hoping to gain entry to the final Dogma at that venue before it closed it's doors forever. The first Dogma I can remember attending was around 12 years ago, when Scan X played. It's a legendary name in Edinburgh's Techno scene and, although I was pretty tired after a week's work, I wanted to be there for the last night. By the time I was only about 15 people short of the door, a bouncer began informing the line of people that the club was full, but you could join another queue for the club upstairs. Ten minutes later I was in the club upstairs, wearing a necklace of fake flowers, holding a can of Red Stripe in each hand and listening to Jerry Lee Lewis singing "Whole Lotta Shakin' Goin' On.". I love old Rock N' Roll records; Phil Spector's Wall Of Sound and Joe Meek stomping on his bathroom floor, and the crowd in attendance seemed to be well into it. Some had a Teddy Boy look going on, and there were a few overly groomed guys walking around with braces holding up their trousers, looking like extras from a saloon scene in an old Western. A lot of the girls were wearing little Oriental print dresses. There was a limbo contest, and even a fairly good recital of John Cooper Clarke's

"Evidently Chicken Town", in between the songs. All the while, though, I could feel the pounding 4/4 kick drum beats from the club below as they shook the floorboards and that's where I wanted to be. I asked a guy manning the cloakroom when it was likely they'd open the door between the two clubs and he said "We're hoping for around 2am.". To me, this seemed like an overly long time away, but a few Red Stripes later, and sometime before 1am, the magic door opened between the two clubs and I made my way straight down the stairs and onto the dance floor. I saw a few familiar faces throughout the night, but I just nodded – who wants to have a chat in the middle of a Techno filled room? There were a few mangled club casualties around, but overall the crowd seemed fairly fresh faced and happy. Sometime around 5:15am the final track of the final night roared out from the rig; "Energy Flash" by Joey Beltram. As the pulsing sub bass rumbled the foundations of the club for the last time, within earshot of Holyrood Palace, I was happy I'd made the effort to be there. Soon after that, I walked home in the early morning Summer sunlight, through quiet streets with my ears still ringing.

I woke up around noon on Sunday feeling a little dazed. My friend, Martin Sweeny, had invited me to an event in Customs Lane, called "Customs & Excess", and it was starting at 2pm. I made it there for around 4pm and the lane was packed full of cheerful, creative, people. Music makers (the dreamers of dreams), video game developers, DJ's, visual arts folk and graphic designers. There was even a guy there who made the beer that everyone was drinking. There was a real community spirit, and Martin has always been great at networking so, before long I was introduced to lots of new and interesting people. Sometime around 8pm, and after I'd had a go on some of the bespoke video games and the weird, Aphex Twin looking, interactive sculpture that was made out of upturned pianos, my old friend Kenny Breaks and I made our way to a nearby pub. Once there we put the world to rights as we necked a few shandies. Then we made our way, via The Port Of Leith, to The Pond bar. Kenny's barbecue parties and DJ events have turned around the fortunes of this particular boozer in recent times. He told me that the bar itself is listed. I was at a quiz night in The Pond on the night that Michael Jackson died, and the bar staff played the whole "Thriller" album after the quiz. My old friend Brendan used to live in the top floor flat above the bar. His living room floor buckled under the weight of his vinyl record collection, and whenever I'd visit his place we would watch the hookers walking up and down Salamander street from his front window, whilst some pristine electronic music played in the background as a soundtrack. In the bar this Sunday night I met a guy called Chris. He was quite hyperactive and funny. He'd once been signed to EMI as a singer songwriter, and he told me stories of how ridiculously long winded the paperwork for such a deal was. Kenny and I left the pub at the very end of the night, and made the short walk to his flat. We listened to one of Kenny's DJ sets and talked about various things, including how a modern version of Trip Hop might be the sound that would best reflect these, rather troubled, political times. After Kenny made us both some cheese on toast with sweet chilli sauce, I hit the road. As I walked through Leith Links my head was buzzing with creative ideas. There were some folk there, in the middle of the night, sitting on benches, alone. I didn't hang around too long pondering "Why?".

Monday and Tuesday found me making music. Instrumental Techno, to be more precise. I haven't made this kind of music for a few years now, but undoubtedly it's the music that I'm best at. It's the genre that I've had the most success with over the years, through airplay and running my own club nights, to the offer of a record deal with RCA. The tracks I've been working on over the past few days are some of the best I've made to date. I think I'm going to release them as an E.P. On my own record label, Unna2ural Wax. Maybe I'll include this written piece as a pdf file, with some new photos, perhaps I'll even include a poem. I'm trying to allow my creativity to come out in any way that it likes. It's a new way of working for me. It's all over the place, but genuinely exciting, as I'm never quite sure what I'm going to have in my hands by the end of a day of making things. For a long time my life has been very structured, and certainly dull. I've made it like that on purpose, as I've been going through a divorce, relocating to

Edinburgh and I've had two new work places over the last nine months or so. That's quite enough to be getting on with for me, so I've tried to create a little structure and stability in my private life while everything else has been up in the air. Wednesday changed that though. It was another night at The Pond, and my old friend Bill Spice was playing a DJ set there for Music Day. There were more creative folk there, and I felt at ease drifting around and chatting to people. I think I must have drank quite a lot, as I seem to have spent a small fortune. I even met a girl. This is despite my recent protests that "I'm happy being single. It means that I can be my own man." and "I always forget who I am when I'm in a relationship." etc, etc. We talked into the small hours, as her flatmate played YouTube videos of gigs that his band had played locally. By noon on Thursday I was walking across Leith Links again. There were different people on the benches in the daylight, and I avoided eye contact with all of them. Could they see my hungover face? Did they realise that I was wearing the clothes I'd nipped out to the pub in yesterday evening?

I spent much of Thursday in bed. This made me feel guilty, as I'd promised Elaine, my live in psychiatrist and landlady, that we'd walk up The Crags beside Arthur's Seat in the afternoon. By evening time I had risen from the dead though. So, we, along with Jodie the dog, went to The Lioness Of Leith and had some food and beers, and all was well with the world again. During our meal I had several Friend Requests on Facebook from people I'd met the previous night at The Pond. They all had fabulous looking lives, with photographs taken in exotic places, flyers for club nights, and all kinds of colourful and interesting stuff going on. In contrast, my profile gives nothing away. I've always deleted posts within a week of creating them, and that goes right back to when I joined Facebook in 2007. I do the same on Twitter, like some kind of online removal man. I guess it's a shame really, as I've had lots of fun over the years, and interactions with all kinds of folk, even some of my heroes, but nonetheless, I've deleted the lot. I just do things differently. I'm OK with that though, I guess it's just a part of being creative. I move onto the next idea pretty quickly, and the thoughts and ideas that I had a couple of weeks ago no longer interest me. I can feel some colour returning to my life though, I could even say that I'm beginning to feel happy again. I know that by this time next week I'll be up to my eyes in work and stress again, but this week off has opened things up for me. I'll not mind calming things down again though. I'm not sure my bank account could withstand a regular hammering like it's taken this week anyway. I might not have a load of cool Facebook posts that describe how much fun I've had this week, but I do have a smile on my actual face – and that's got to be better. Tonight I'm going to take my camera down into Leith and photograph some of those old shop fronts, the one's that have been closed for decades. I think they look great. They haven't been deleted, yet.

LIBERATION LOOPHOLE

01.09.2017

Words by Stephen Clarke 1980

Music by The Justified Ancients Of Mu Mu

Earlier this afternoon I was contacted by Welcome To The Dark Ages. They wanted to know if I'd be interested in writing about the recent return of The Justified Ancients Of Mu Mu, from the perspective of someone who wasn't in Liverpool between Wednesday the 23rd and Saturday the 26th of August, 2017, and wasn't one of the 400 "volunteers" who paid a hundred quid each to be there. I was perfect for the job, with my skill set matching their requirements to the letter. Being in such a strong position, I quickly managed to negotiate a fee of £0,000,000 for my services, and within minutes the job was mine.

I was 7 years old when Bill Drummond and Jimmy Cauty first topped the charts, as The Timelords. I lived in Belfast at the time, and I can remember the sounds of army helicopters, gun battles and bomb explosions a lot more clearly than any of the Pop records of that time. Once their "Stadium House Trilogy" songs were on the radio though, I was a bit older, and getting into all of the hip new sounds that my Dad hated. The first KLF song I played, repeatedly, was the All Bound For Mu Mu Land version of Justified & Ancient. This mix doesn't feature "The First Lady Of Country", Tammy Wynette. It had Maxine Harvey on vocal duties, and a running time of almost 8 minutes. As far as I can recall, it was the second track on a Rave compilation CD I'd bought with some money I'd been given for my birthday, and I can't remember any of the other songs on the disk. I just kept playing the same song, over and over. I'd never heard anything like it before (or since). It had, amongst a maelstrom of other noises, a sound like a school bell or a fire alarm running through it, and a rap about an ice cream van. When it finally drifted away all I was left with were questions. I mean, where are the Rivers Of Life? Do you need a licence to fish there? Where on earth is Mu Mu Land? I'd heard that the last train had left an hour ago, but I was hoping there would be a replacement bus service, or a connecting flight that I could catch to take me there.

Sometime after that girls, and underage drinking, began to creep into my life, and that early, magical, rush provided by brilliant Pop music began to drift away, never again to be captured in quite the same way. It happens to us all, I guess. Just like you'll never forget your first kiss, you'll never forget the first time a great song takes your brain to another dimension. For Bill Drummond, that song is Strawberry Fields Forever by The Beatles, and for me, it's Justified & Ancient (All Bound For Mu Mu Land) by The KLF. To be honest, the rest of their activities completely passed me by. That is until I bought a copy of Bill Drummond's book "45", a few years after it was originally published. To this day, it remains my favourite publication of all time, and, in fact, I can tell you exactly where I was when I was first reading it.

On the second day of November 2002 I was being driven on a coach from Belfast to Prague, via the Irish and North sea's. I was reading the chapter Towers, Tunnels And Elderflower Wine as the coach headed towards Bill Drummond's old stomping ground, Newton Stewart. Suddenly there was a diversion, both in the book and off the route the coach I was on was supposed to be taking, and then, all of a sudden, both I, in the present, and Bill, when he wrote the chapter (9th of September, 1998), are in the village of Minnigaff. Then my mobile phone began to ring. I didn't recognise the number, but I answered the call and heard; "Hello, this is Bill Drummond. Is that Stephen?". What followed was the most surreal, let's say, 23 minutes, of my life. I'd posted Bill a letter about a week, or so, previously, saying that I was enjoying his book, and that The KLF should think about putting out a Greatest Hits CD (This was the peak time for CD selling, profit wise. Just before Napster, and, well, you know all the rest). Bill said he had just arrived home from Belfast. He'd been repairing his Curfew Tower, and had found himself at a loose end, but he didn't have my contact details with him. So, he thought he'd phone me now that he was home and catching up on business. I asked about The KLF and he said "I feel that I have totally left the music business. That stuff doesn't interest me any more. But, I'm still friends with Jimmy. We met up last year actually. We we're thinking of maybe doing something with our film footage. We have loads of film, and we actually started working on it.". All the while we were talking I could hear his kids playing in the background. It was a lovely, easy, conversation. The kind of chat that you'd hope you could have with an artist who's work you admire, but how you often dread that they'd actually be an arsehole if you ever spoke to them in real life (In fact, in "45", Bill does have that exact kind of, soul destroying, conversation with his own hero, Peter Green). At the end of the chat we both wished each other a happy Christmas and said goodbye. As the coach I was sitting in continued to trundle on through the Scottish countryside, I gazed out of the window and smiled, for a long time. In the years that followed I exchanged the odd email with Bill, and in 2008 he asked me if I'd like to write a Score for his project, The 17. This is what I wrote;

SCORE 338. DREAM

Sit in a place where journeys begin. Look around you for sixteen people you connect with. Think about these connections and absorb them deeply. Close your eyes. Clear your mind of all thoughts. There will be noise. Your body will turn the volume up. The sixteen people you connect with share this feeling. They will each contact you through sound. Focus your mind on making the greatest music you have ever heard. You will believe that this is possible for you. You will feel this possibility on every level. You will feel it as if it has already happened. The greatest music of all time is inside you. Wake up. The sixteen people you have connected with will have moved on. It will be time for you to begin your journey.

In the years that followed I had a life. I ran some successful club nights in Edinburgh and had a few of my songs played on Radio 1. Then I moved to a tiny cottage on a large country estate in rural Perthshire, during the worst winter in living memory, and one of my neighbours was Dougie Maclean, who wrote the famous Scottish song "Caledonia". I've had some of the honey from the bees he keeps on my toast. You can do things like eat your neighbours honey when you live out in the countryside. I got married. I got divorced. The seasons changed, and the years rolled by. All the while I'd occasionally check out what Bill Drummond and James Cauty were up to. I read Bill's books, and I visited Jimmy's Aftermath Dislocation Principle when it came to Edinburgh, where I'm now living, last year. However, all the while there was silence on anything relating to their previous work as The KLF, K Foundation, Justified Ancients Of Mu Mu etc. This was, roughly, due to them signing a contract relating to a 23 year moratorium on their activities, in gold ink, on the windscreen of a Nissan Bluebird that they had hired in Aviemore, then driven to Cape Wrath, Scotland. After that, they painted the contract all over the car, before pushing the vehicle over a clifftop and walking away into oblivion, or London, as it's more commonly known. All the while, their loyal fans would tweet each other occasionally, share the odd home made remix, talk about A Riot In A Jam Jar, or The Soup Line, and basically wait around, listening to rare albums on YouTube, whilst they read the odd unofficial book, or watched a fan made video, about their old heroes. It was a long and quiet wait for all of us old, ageing, KLF fans. I wonder how many of the good men and women of Mu we lost along the way?

Then, suddenly, on January 5th, 2017, a single poster appeared on a wall in Hackney, London. At long, long last, this was the sign that K watchers the world over had been waiting for. Under the logo for the duo's company K2 PLANT HIRE Ltd (The name under which Drummond and Cauty had once planned to "Fix" Stonehenge, and "Get it working again", as a millennial gift to the nation) the poster read; "2017: What the Fuck Is Going On?" (A very pertinent question, for a lot of people, after the remarkable global events of 2016). It then rambled on for a few paragraphs before delivering a killer couple of lines that would set the internet ablaze for weeks to come; "The Justified Ancients Of Mu Mu are currently at work in their light industrial unit. This work will not be made public until the 23rd of August 2017.". Over the coming weeks, and months, rumours began circulating that this "Work" was going to be a sculpture, and that there would definitely be no new music made by the duo. Then, another poster appeared. It's job was to let the world know that "K2 Plant Hire Ltd present 2023 - a trilogy by The Justified Ancients Of Mu Mu". So, it wasn't going to be a sculpture then? It was going to be a book. A book published by Faber & Faber, no less. So, probably a descent book, but still, a book. I mean, we've only been waiting 23 sodding years guys! Soon after, yet another poster appeared, declaring that The JAMs would be "unearthing aspects of the 2023 trilogy across Liverpool from 00:23 on the 23rd to 23:23 on the 27th Aug 2017.". At least this poster had the Pyramid Blaster logo on it, even if it was probably advertising a three day book reading. Maybe Bill would be doing one of his talks, whilst Jimmy made a 1:87 scale sculpture of the Pyramid Blaster live on stage, and then they'd set fire to both the book and the model while all around them yawned, or something like that. I mean, they're getting on a bit now.

Maybe that's all they could manage. It was 2017, and all was dull again. That was until a DVD+R, with the words "2023 The Triptych Trailer 1", scrawled on it with a black Sharpie, was found stuck to a wall in London, with black duct tape. Within 24 hours this, insane, trailer was on YouTube. It featured, amongst other things, a beeping alarm clock noise, floating, sliced grapefruit, a revolving tall pyramid that looked like The Shard, London - except it was hovering over a wheat field, with two dark figures wearing long hats and carrying walking sticks, gazing at this revolving object. Then, suddenly, The Shard In The Sky (That's where I'm gonna go when I die. When I die and they lay me to rest, gonna go to the place that's the best...) was ablaze. Then, ladies and gentlemen, we were floating in space. A sleeping satellite told us all to FUUK-UP. Starbucks Yoko was there too, before Vladimir Putin appeared, sitting on a throne with a fox by his side, in front of an image from Stanley Kubrick's A Clockwork Orange (The intense gaze of chief Droog, Malcolm McDowell, fixing us all with a menacing intent), as the words "Art War" flashed. Then we watched a fox on the prowl, walking through the city streets as The Shard burned in the background (This was before the Grenfell Tower fire in London, and watching this video now as I make these notes, is actually a bit shocking). We could see graffiti on a wall, and it read "Kick out The JAMs". This was all followed by some floating green leaves with the Facebook logo on them, before the video ended. By now, The Justified Ancients Of Mu Mu had been asking us all the same question for 30 years. At the end of "2023 The Triptych Trailer 1", all we could do was ask them that very same question; 2017: WHAT THE FUCK IS GOING ON?

As the Summer of 2017 began, we were all treated to the site of The JAMs, who had now become slightly freaky looking scarecrows, as they stood in various locations. The media began to softly tickle the nation again, and more details began to emerge of what would be happening in Liverpool in August. The JAMs were going to be launching their new book in the News From Nowhere bookshop, on Bold Street. A few years ago I, and my ex-wife, had both tried our very best to get hold of Bill Drummond's book "100" from this shop, and from any other place we could think of, but, alas, we failed. If any kind hearted readers have a copy of this book, I would dearly love to read it. Maybe it belongs to your partner, and you don't like your partner any more? Perhaps you're an over worked and underpaid teacher, with a disruptive class. Maybe they could copy the book out for me during detention? Perhaps you are Bill Drummond, and you could email it to me as a PDF? My name is Stephen Clarke 1980, and you can find me on the outerweb. Anyway, tickets for their upcoming return went on sale, for £100 a pop, on the 23rd of July, and they sold like hot sheep. All were sold in 23 seconds. The rest of the world, myself included, were assured this particular revolution would not be televised. There were no invited media, there was no guest list and there would be no red carpet.

I've just realised that there's already a healthy word count on this piece, and I haven't even scratched the surface of Welcome To The Dark Ages yet. That, in fact, is what this blog post is supposed to be about, after all. My sense of humour, being what it is, means that I would quite like to end this script right here, and tell you that that's what it was like not being there. However, that's simply not true. While I've been typing up the words you've been reading so far, I've also been scrawling down 4 pages of handwritten notes on what it was like, as a long time KLF fan, watching Welcome To The Dark Ages unfold from a distance. The temptation, of course, is to try and describe the events as they unfolded on the ground. However, I, along with the bulk of the population, simply wasn't there, and that's just not the way the information from this, rather mammoth, event tended to reach us. There are plenty of "The 400" who have written about Welcome To The Dark Ages, as they happened (Day One; We did this, then that. Day Two; No sleep.... etc), and for that, I, and many others will be eternally grateful. From this point onwards, I'm going to try to tell the truth about the event, as I saw it, as it came to me. The emotions that I felt, and the ideas that went through my mind as I watched Welcome To The Dark Ages; The return, after 23 long years in the wilderness, of the band that I love more than any other band in the eternal history of time.

I'm going to begin by saying that Welcome To The Dark Ages was, without a shadow of a doubt, a live performance by the artists forever known as The Justified Ancients Of Mu Mu. I know they don't like being called The KLF, and they've always thought of themselves as The JAMs, even when they were The KLF. However, they simply don't get a choice when it comes to this one. Every press piece, TV slot, radio broadcast and Tweet worldwide, called this The Return Of The KLF. So, that's what it was guys. Sorry, it's already out there, in the big, bad, world now, and there's nothing that any of us, Bill and Jimmy included, can do about it. The good news for fans is that, despite The JAMs request for no broadcast quality equipment, the outerweb has been absolutely filled to the brim with hours worth of footage, and photos, from this remarkable, once in a lifetime, three day happening. I, personally, have downloaded over 4GB worth of videos and photographs taken over the course of this event. The bulk of these were found by searching YouTube and Twitter for The KLF or #KLF, then checking out what had been uploaded in the last 24 hours. I really didn't find too much when searching for The JAMs. In fact, at many times during the three day event I was more likely to find fresh footage and photos by searching for the, at the time imaginary, band Badger Kull, than I was by searching for The JAMs. However, The JAMs, being The JAMs probably don't want to be sodding found anyway. They like a bit of isolation, in order to get to work - these pyramids don't build themselves you know. Writing that reminds me of the answerphone message at the beginning of their old, strange, film "Waiting". It's basically a video of Bill and Jimmy on the island of Jura, giving KLF fans instructions on what they themselves, along with their fans, would be spending the next couple of decades doing; Pissing about, and gazing into the middle distance. Anyway, the answerphone message says things like, "I've been trying to get a hold of The KLF.... I need to get a hold of The KLF....". Well, that's what the world's media were trying to do during Welcome To The Dark Ages, but, in the main, they failed. They managed to get a couple of books stamped, and then they, rather lazily, dug up a few, old, irrelevant, Pop videos from the previous century, giggled and rolled their eyes about the money burning whilst dressed in sharp suits, and then moved on to the weather forecast. The fans, however, got the lot. The KLF live on stage, The JAMs dead in the streets (Who killed them this time?), and the Rites Of Mu(Mufication). Everything they've been dreaming about, and waiting years for, and more.

I spent much of Tuesday the 22nd of August, 2017, following everyone on Twitter who were discussing things like what time the love was going to start, what time the last train was going to leave and who could bring home a dime. By 11:55pm I had live feeds running and updates pouring in from every person who was standing within a 23 mile radius of Bold Street. At 11:58 a series of huge, orange, armoured cars entered the area. They had large, black, K's on the side, and were being driven by a masked gang, wearing high visibility vests. A police helicopter appeared in the night sky, just about visible through the blinding aurora borealis. A cop was hanging out of the side of the chopper, holding a megaphone, and instructing the enormous crowd to go back to their homes, that this was an illegal gathering, and that there was nothing to see here. "Go home and watch the rolling news channels. They will keep you all informed about what is truly important in this world. Please remember to lock your doors and fear your neighbours at all times." he said, in a calm, strong and stable voice. The swelling crowd, mostly, stood their ground. A single, brave, and almost broken, civilian (A beautiful, young, girl. Her head shaven by the Protectors Of The State) stepped forward into a small clearing. Then, as the strong beam of light from the chopper shone directly into her dazzling, weeping, eyes, and her body trembled she abruptly raised her fist to the stars and screamed "If you don't like what they're going to do, You better not stop them 'cause they're coming through!". The copper in the chopper scanned her faced with a long range video lens, and then fucked off. A few people started fleeing the scene, fearing for their safety, but they soon came back when they got a sudden, midnight, craving for ice cream. One crazed fan had climbed the rigging of an old Viking long ship that had just pulled up. Ford Timelord arrived, with a fresh paint job, and raced down Bold Street, doing his best To Serve And Protect the Children Of Mu, and clearing the way for the return of his old pals. High above Liverpool the International Space Station was passing slowly through the night sky. It was hard to make out the audio on some of the periscope feeds, but the ISS did clearly declare "Poised for main engine start.". The feed from bold street was crystal clear though, and Ford Timelord replied, "Roger that, copy". At that moment the bells of a nearby church began to ring, indicating that it was now the 23rd of August, 2017. The ISS said "Okay Liverpool, we'll give you a countdown; Twenty three, twenty two, twenty one...". At this point the crowd were seriously losing their shit. Some people were fainting, others were holding sheep aloft and pointing them at the church. The ISS continued "Four, three, two, one...". Just then, the figure who had climbed the rigging of the long ship appeared, just briefly, to be the King Of Pop! The crowd roared as he yelled, "TURN UP THE STROBE!". At that exact moment every periscope stream went down for one 23rd of a second. When the broadcast returned, the Viking long ship was gone, the aurora had cleared, taking Michael with it, and the ISS was flashing the largest strobe light in the galaxy. Everything happened so fast that it was hard to keep up, but suddenly, there they were, our long, long, lost heroes! I fainted briefly, then regained Konsciousness, as Rockman Rock and King Boy D raced into Bold Street in their famous Ice Kream Van to perform live, as The KLF, for the first time in 23 years! The old van was as knackered as our heroes looked, and they were all leaking burnt £50 notes. An effigy of Tammy Wynette was resting peacefully inside a beautiful Koffin that The JAMs had made especially for her. Grown men and women were weeping openly and holding hands, as children, with rhino horns attached to their heads, laughed, giggled, and danced around, chanting "Mu Mu!", and "Bring home a dime, Make mine a "99"!". King Boy D impulsively started playing The KLF's sampler, live, for the first time since the Helter Skelter Rave in Chipping Norton in 1989. He was older now, for sure, but he still had that twinkle in his eye, and with his maniacal grin and missing tooth he seemed happy to be mesmerising the crowd again, plus he was totally fucking smashing the What Time Is Love riff. Whatever it was he used to have, well, he still had it. By the time he was mashing it up with Justified & Ancient the Mersey was filled to the brim with dancing perch. Rockman had been playing it pretty cool up to this point, tapping out the beats flawlessly on the steering wheel of the Ice Kream Van. Then he promptly stopped the van and handed his aviator shades through the window to Gimpo. Suddenly the whole world fell silent to listen to Rockman speak. "Any chance you could get the press out of the way mate?", said Jimmy, softly. "No worries, pal." said Gimpo, who then turned and walked to the front of the Ice Kream Van with his arms outstretched like the messiah, and the press quickly retreated back into the gutters. King Boy D rolled down his window, and held the hand of a trembling fan, I think it was Scarlett Johansson. Then Bill, in his thickest, deepest, Scottish accent, with a hint of reverb, said "And from somewhere, I hear...". Scarlett held Bill close, and mumbled something incomprehensible, but clearly loving and affectionate into his ear. Bill turned his face away and, with a single tear rolling down his right cheek, he pressed play on the old sampler that he'd once pissed off ABBA with. The night air instantly filled with the sound of "'O sole mio (Famous Again With The Headlines Coming Up Remix)". It was at that moment that the most iconic photograph of this millennium was taken. The one with the Ice Kream Van in the middle of Bold Street, with The KLF and Tammy all aboard, all aboard, a-woah-ho, all smiling away, with "The Boys Are Back In Town" written on top of the van in Ukrainian. It's the photograph that was on the front page of every major global news paper for 23 weeks after the event. By now The JAMs were pretty tired, and it was time for them to take their meds. So, they went into the book shop to drink some tea and stamp anything that was put in front of them, their eyes not being quite what they used to be. They were stamping books, boobs, Scottish Wild Cats, a signed photo of Tony Wilson, Pete Waterman's arm, all kinds of stuff. Once their meds had kicked in though, Bill took the time to enquire politely to the News From Nowhere staff, to check if they still had a copy of "100" lying around that they could send to Stephen Clarke 1980 immediately, as a special request. "Even on PDF", Jimmy expanded, "We like him. He's cool with us.".

OK, OK. There might be a few half truths in the above paragraph, but to me, watching The Return Of The KLF from afar FELT like that. You and I both know the story of this band, and the myths that surround them. However, a lot of people don't. Maybe they missed them first time around, or they were too old, or not born yet by the time The JAMs were playing games with the universe. The story of their strange return was all over the television news by breakfast time. I mean, can you imagine what it must have been like to be a teenager who watched that before they headed off to school, or a stock broker off to work in the city? An example story, from the BBC; "You might remember that back in the early 1990's, the British Electronic duo KLF churned out hit after hit, with songs like 3AM Eternal and Justified and Ancient. But then, in 1994 they burned a million pounds in cash and disappeared, and just before that they said they would come back in 23 years time. At the stroke of midnight last night that was when the 23 years were up; KLF reappeared - They did it!". I'm pretty sure the reaction to stories like that, in houses up and down the country, indeed, throughout the world, would have been just as The JAMs would have wanted it; Thousands of people, of every race, creed and colour, staring at their TV screens and saying "What the fuck?" in unison. So, while "The 400" were tucking into their non-Full English breakfast the next morning, and waiting around to get allocated jobs and all of that shite, the real magic was happening back out in the unreal world.

As far as me calling the event a live KLF show, well, of course it wasn't, in the traditional sense. However, if you're thinking traditionally about The KLF then, frankly, you're doing it wrong. The KLF were never a live act. Of course they could put on sensational, and memorable, TV performances and create colossal Pop videos, but you were never going to catch them playing your local arena, and I sincerely hope that they never do. And yes, I know they played live with Echo And The Bunnymen in Bootle, and then there's the Helter Skelter rave in Chipping Norton where they showered the crowd with Scottish pound notes, with "We love you" scrawled on them, and there was the Extreme Noise Terror show at The Brits. However, I'm not sure I'd really like to see them play The Pyramid Stage at Glastonbury (even if it has them written all over it). These are the kinds of things that real bands do, and I don't think The KLF are a real band. I think they are a great art project, run by The JAMs. Bill is, obviously, the project manager, and Jimmy is the artist that makes the piece, and then they both take their finished product out of their studio, or their light industrial unit, and present it to the world in the weirdest way possible, not for our benefit, but just to make themselves laugh. Just a great pair of old friends that like a giggle, and a walk around the town together with their pockets stuffed full of in jokes (They've always valued in jokes more than money). That doesn't mean I'm having a go at their music, from What Time Is Love (Pure Trance Version), through Chill Out, to Build A Fire, I love them all. It's just that I see them as great pieces of art, rather than a bunch of songs I'd like to see them perform every night for 3 months on a tour of Europe in the shape of a K, with every gig starting at 23:23 local time. That said, what "The 400" witnessed was undoubtedly a live KLF show, in the non-traditional sense. Bill and Jimmy did arrive in their Ice Kream Van playing a medley of What Time Is Love, Justified & Ancient and 'O sole mio. I'm sticking to my Tammy Wynette in the Koffin theory, as it's the first thought I had when I saw the Koffin in the back of the Ice Kream Van, and I'm a man who trusts his gut feelings. I've heard other people saying that the Koffin contained an effigy of James Brown. If that's the case, then he'll always be "The First Lady Of Country" to me. Then there were the two Koffins carried into the K2 gig, to the epic sounds of Jerusalem On The Moors by The Justified Ancients Of Mu Mu. Again, it's obvious that Bill and Jimmy were inside these two koffins throughout the whole gig. So, they could both be centre stage and lie back and enjoy their own funeral. This was then followed by the internet sensation of Jarvis Cocker Joins The JAMs / MuMufied & Ancient, or whatever the fuuk that was. It was pointed out pretty quickly why The KLF and

Jarvis Cocker were so well matched; They had both caused anarchy at The Brit Awards, a mere four years apart. Admittedly, "They called me up in Sheffield town. They said "Jarvis, stand by The JAMs."", was a pretty cool moment. I felt a bit like Rocky Balboa dancing about on top of those steps in Philadelphia, when he sang that. KLF fans will have noticed that this particular performance contains the beautiful breakdown from Last Train To Trancentral ("The di-na-ni-na-ni-na-ni-na, Big Country bit", as Bill Drummond described it to Tom Robinson in 2004). I must admit here, dear reader, that when this section of the track kicked in, and Jarvis began to pray, and because it was Bill and Jimmy's funeral, and.... Well, anyway, I welled up, and I thought it was worth the 23 year wait just for that moment alone. Then, at The Funeral Pyre, where Bill and Jimmy torched their own Koffins, "The 400" got a live performance of America No More (Just The Pipe Band) by The KLF, whilst Bill and Jimmy walked around a burning funeral pyre, representing The People's Pyramid, with The KLF's iconic rhino horns on their heads. Now, seriously, if you can't see that as the finest live KLF show of all time, then we have issues. Then, of course, we had Badger Kull and, their one and only 3 minute song, "Toxteth Day Of The Dead.". Again, this live performance kicked off with an introduction made very much to sound like the legendary MC5 sample that The KLF famously used in their 1991 hit, Stadium House, remake of What Time Is Love. As for the Badger Kull song itself, it reminded me of the type of songs that Bill Drummond came up with when he invented a load of fake bands in Finland, then released them on his own label Kalevala Records. In fact, at the end of this whole evening DJ Food ended his set with one of those very records, "In The Ghetto" by The Blizzard King. Personally, I was so into the Badger Kull idea that I recorded two tracks myself, under the Badger Kull name, and uploaded them to the outerweb. They were basically remakes of old KLF songs, with silly updates (Badger noises, President Trump, Ice Kream Van chimes). The first track was called "What Chimes With Love (Live At TranSETTral)", the second one was "America: What Time Is Liverpool (Just The Piped Badgers)". The hysteria for all things Badger Kull related, meant that these tracks were played over 700 times in one day, and I'd only alerted the public about them via a single Tweet.

Apart from us being told that The JAMs wouldn't be performing any music, which, as I've explained, isn't true - they did, we were also informed that there would be no new songs from them either, this too was bollocks. The new JAMs song is called "Fuuk The World (How To Have A Christmas Number One The Easy Way)", and it was the first Drummond/Cauty musical collaboration since their 2K "Fuck The Millennium" project in 1997. Just like the 2k performance, The JAMs themselves were made up as a pair of grumpy old men for the live show. This time, instead of a brass band and some striking dockers providing the audio content, our heroes put together a group of talented members of The 400, called Band Aid 2023. Now, if you're going to try and tell me that this song was not a Drummond/Cauty song, then riddle me this one Batman; Without Bill Drummond and Jimmy Cauty giving Band Aid 2023 the opportunity to make a Christmas Number One in a bombed out church in Liverpool, after providing them with words from a book they'd just published, would this, great, song exist? It's filled with wonderful lines, like "Selling arms around the world, at Dark Age time.", "It's Mu Mu time, but What The Fuuk Is Going On?", "There's a world outside your boathouse.", and "There won't be perch in Merseyside this Christmas time.". OK, maybe they didn't write the tune, but The Timelords didn't write the tune to their number one either, did they? In all honesty, I think this performance is one of the best things to come out of Welcome To The Dark Ages. Like lots of the events that happened over those three days in Liverpool, it was very unexpected. But, this might have been one of the few things that even The JAMs themselves didn't see coming, and they loved it. You can see them nudging each other and smiling as they read the lyrics. You can watch them rocking with laughter, and nodding their heads in approval when the beat kicks in. They've both always loved, and understood, Pop music, and that was exactly what this was. It's perfect, absolutely perfect, and entertaining, and funny. To further back up my claim, I'll quote something that Bill Drummond said about the duo's first number one record, "Doctorin' The Tardis" by The

Timelords; "We were rolling around on the floor laughing because we knew it was a number one single, which we wanted. Wouldn't you? But it was more an act of celebration than cynicism.". Now, go and watch the clip of "Band Aid 2023 - Christmas No1" if it's still floating around the outerweb in whatever year it is that you're reading this, and have a look at Bill Drummond and Jimmy Cauty as they listen to the first playback of their new song. It might have been nearly 30 years since they first rolled around on the floor laughing while listening to one of their creations by then, but their reaction to a great piece of Pop music remained the same. The only difference is that this time we all got to laugh along with them, and it was absolutely glorious. One of my Twitter friends, Paul, who was a member of The 400, agrees; "I was right at the front and every time I glanced across at them they were both pissing themselves laughing.". I think that's one of the things about Bill and Jimmy, they are a pair of like minded guys with a great sense of humour. We're all just lucky that they are also exceptionally talented artists as well, because we can get to join in on the fun too. If you're ever feeling a bit low, have a listen to The JAMs "The Queen And I" (Unless you're a member of ABBA), or "Whitney Joins The JAMs". I mean even Tammy singing about an ice cream van should put a smile on your face. Why sheep? Why perch? I love that when the definitive answer to why they burned £1,000,000 23 years ago was given to them by The 400, their response was "Whatever". They really are teenagers at heart, and despite Bill Drummond's 10 commandments of art including; "Don't come the rebel", I have absolutely no doubt whatsoever that a rebel is exactly what he is. But, I'm sure if I brought it up with him, his reply would be "Accept the contradictions.". I thought the pair of them giving the replica of Ford Timelord a fresh white paint job was really funny. The owner of the car didn't seem too impressed, but if he watched the film The White Room, that's what they did to the original Ford Timelord anyway. The owner has since cleaned the paint off, but I think he should have let The JAMs finish their job. I mean, who else on earth could say, "Oh, The KLF? Yeah I know, they were great weren't they? They painted my car.". Personally I thought the touch up job was cooler, and should have been donated to the city of Liverpool, for it's safe storage atop a plinth in the centre of an area of outstanding natural beauty.

By the end of Welcome To The Dark Ages, we had all learned that the sculpture that The JAMs had been working on was called The People's Pyramid. At the time of it's completion it will stand at 23 feet in height, and be built from 34,592 household bricks. Each of these bricks will contain 23 grams of cremated ashes from willing individual's. The name given to this process is MuMufication. I've known that Jimmy Cauty has wanted to become a house brick for quite some time. Between the years 2003 and 2012, Bill Drummond ran a website called My Death, where users could sign up and provide details of what they'd like to have happen in the event of their death; funeral plans etc. Anyway, Jimmy Cauty wrote, "I want to be cremated and the ashes made into a house brick. If Bill or Gimpo outlive me they will know where to go, if not any brick maker will do.". As we all know, he's been calling himself Rockman Rock for years. The White Room version of Justified & Ancient even

includes the line "Rock Man, he's just made of bricks.".
The ashes from their burning of £1,000,000 on the Isle Of
Jura on the 23rd of August, 1994, were also, as every
schoolboy knows, made into a house brick. There's a
common British phrase, relating to money, that says
"Invest in bricks and mortar, and you can't go wrong.". I
have a theory that at some point in the early 90's, when
The KLF were rolling in cash, someone gave the lads this
common bit of advice, but after playing live with Extreme
Noise Terror their ears weren't in great shape, and The
JAMs heard this as "Invest yourselves in bricks and
mortuaries, and you can't be gone.". Other than
MuMufication, The JAMs, or CCCD (Callender, Callender,
Cauty & Drummond Undertakers) have a few other
services on offer. If you'd like them to build you a Koffin
For Life, or K4L, made to order, from packing case
material, it will cost you £999. However, my favourite
service is "Ice Kream Van as Hearse with The Justified
Ancients of Mu Mu as driver and knitter to carry a Koffin
4 Life containing body to a funeral – £9,999 (UK only).".
Frankly, I think that's an absolute bargain to be driven by
your favourite Pop stars to your funeral in their world

famous Ice Kream Van. I mean, what's the going rate for The Orb to get you to the church on time? That lot don't even have an Ice Kream Van. I mean, try getting a Little Fluffy Cloud to carry you along to a funeral the next time you're in need of one. I guarantee you you'll have a solid excuse for being late. I wonder if Bill will be putting 23g of himself into The People's Pyramid, or if the whole Drummond, and nothing but the whole Drummond, will be tipped into the Penkiln Burn when the time comes? (By the way, Bill, if you're reading this, I miss the Penkiln Burn Website. in particular the work you were doing with barbers. If you made that into a book, I'd buy it. If not, just send it to me in a PDF along with "100", and that'll be fine.).

I've read a lot of Tweets over the last few days from members of The 400 who have been trying to decompress. Getting back to their day jobs, thinking that if they tried to explain to their co-workers what they've just been getting up to in Liverpool, they just wouldn't get it. Some are finding it hard to get back to life, back to reality, others have tattoos relating to a band that once played a song for 3 minutes and then disappeared forever. They've all joined a rather elite group of people who have worked with The KLF, and I'm not just talking about now. The members of The 400 are all just as important as every dancer who ever took part in one of the bands epic videos, or Top Of The Pops appearances. Just as significant as every robed journalist who took part in The Rites Of Mu, and just as crucial as every sheep who lay down (and the one that stood up) for the cover photo of "Chill Out". You see, at the time that all of these events happened, those people involved probably felt the same as well. Years from now, members of The 400 will be asked, at length, in late night pub conversations about what they got up to that time they did that thing with The KLF. Other times, they themselves might want to show off about it, and be greeted by faces that just don't get it, and who's only reply will be "What the fuck's going on?". I like the way it all ends up as precious old, grainy, footage making it's way around YouTube for obsessive fans to watch on their day's away from the grindstone. For all of The 400's worries about how the event was reported, and how the magic just wasn't captured. Try not to worry about it. Even the burning of £1,000,000 was hardly reported anywhere at the time. These events become whispers, and strange tales told with bits missing, or facts got wrong. That's OK. I think it's exactly how The Jams want it to be. Their real strength lies in mystery, and this is how mystery is created. If they'd filmed it all professionally, and released a DVD packed with extras, just in time for Christmas, it would be great. But, then again, it would also be shit. It would become something you could walk into a music shop and buy, and that is not what KLF is about. Some people get it, and some people don't. I love the old line from the Saint Etienne song, Mario's Cafe; "Eubank wins the fight, and did you see the KLF last night?". For me, that's what they are, at their best; a great topic of conversation down your local greasy spoon cafe. Just as I hope that some schoolkids minds were blown when they watched the BBC breakfast news, and heard for the first time that some band burned a million quid, I hope that there were plenty of truckers, and shelf stackers (like me), and all kinds of everyday Joe's who just had a little chat down the cafe about "Those fucking nutters! Did you see that ice cream van? There was a bloody coffin in the back of the sodding thing!","Yeah I know. I saw a video with all these zombies in robes at a Pulp gig. What the fuck's going on?".

I don't think the work of The 400 has finished, it may have only just begun. In the words of Bill Drummond, "Don't join the dots.". It's your job now to print the legend, be mysterious, speak the truth, tell lies, and watch the magic and mystery of the event, that you just helped create, grow over time. The JAMs gave you the seeds, plant them wisely. Like I wrote earlier, I've downloaded over 4GB worth of videos and photographs from Welcome To The Dark Ages. I have all of the videos in one folder of my computer, and I was going to match them up with the timetable of events that The JAMs gave out, in order that when I play them it all has a structure and a flow to it. A documentary style accuracy to it that makes sense. However, I made a wee playlist earlier from the videos that just played them all, one after the other, in alphabetical order. This meant that they were all out of sequence, and they didn't make too much sense at all at times. In fact, it was a bit like watching Pulp Fiction for the first time; You don't really have a clue who these people are, or what they're doing, and it jumps around a lot. But, the dialogue is cool, and the way it jumps around means you're going to have to watch it a few times to really work out What The Fuck it's all about. Then every now and then, suddenly one of those brilliant, memorable, moments from the event would come on. A classic scene you'll be quoting to your friends for years, and it's just magical. So, I'm tempted to keep them all as they came to me, just as they would have came to everyone else on the planet who wasn't at Welcome To The Dark Ages; A strange, crazy, amazing, jaw dropping, confusing, exhausting, exciting, tear jerking, hands in the air, rocking, mystical, trance like, ritualistic, badger filled, Christmas song in August, rhino horned, cop car painting, skull faced procession, that had something to do with a dead perch, Starbucks, Yoko Ono, traffic cones and ragworts in shopping trolleys. Jarvis Cocker was there at one point, in a choir of skulls. There were stamped books, cups of tea and a bombed out church. Oh, and the whole thing started in an Ice Kream Van and ended in a pyramid made out of 34,592 dead people. Yeah, as you can see, it's going to be a really simple experience to process and then relate to people. Either that, or you may end up on some kind of ward with just a toothbrush and a badly designed gown for company. It could go either way, really.

I've called this blog Liberation Loophole, because in my 2001 edition of The Manual (How To Have A Number One The Easy Way), Bill Drummond wrote an afterword called "In Praise Of Council Homes" (It's also in his book, "45"). In the piece he discusses the list of band names Bill and Jimmy listed for themselves at the front of the first edition of The Manual in 1988. These were; Lord Rock And Time Boy, The Timelords, Rockman Rock And Kingboy D, The Justified Ancients Of Mu Mu, The Jams, The KLF, The Fall and The Forever Ancients Liberation Loophole. He says that The Forever Ancients Liberation Loophole is a name that they never got to use. "It still feels like we're holding back on it, keeping it in reserve for when things get totally out of control and we need to make a quick escape.". Well, I reckon since Bill and Jimmy aren't using the Liberation Loophole just now, they'll not mind lending it to us for a bit (They're nice like that). So, if you find that things are getting totally out of control and you need to make a quick escape, you now know what to do.

If you're still confused about things, and really not sure What The Fuck is Going On? The only further information I can give you, are some words that were once delivered, with a powerful strength and conviction, by a man named Jervis Ricardo Alfonso Lyte (30 April 1967 – 8 March 2013). He was better known to the world as Ricardo Da Force, or to KLF fans as Ricardo Lyte (He is a credited performer on 3AM Eternal, Last Train To Trancentral and Justified And Ancient). Anyway, sometime way back in the early 1990's, this man walked into a recording studio with The KLF, got himself inside the vocal booth, put a pair of headphones on, stepped up to the microphone, opened his mouth and gave you the only answer that you'll ever need to reach for the next time you're feeling baffled by your experiences at Welcome To The Dark Ages, or, if you're worried that the rest of the world just doesn't get it; Try to "Chill Out", give yourself some "Space", and remember;

"THIS IS WHAT KLF IS ABOUT,
ALSO KNOWN AS THE JUSTIFIED ANCIENTS OF MU MU,
FURTHERMORE KNOWN AS THE JAMS."

OVER AND OUT.

You have been reading "Liberation Loophole" by Stephen Clarke 1980.

You can find Stephen Clarke 1980 by searching for him.

MESSAGE ENDS.

NIL BY ARSE

25.09.2017

My health has been failing for some time now. I began a
new job in March, which is basically a shelf stacking gig.
I walk 50 minutes to get there, work my ass off during my
9 hour shift, then walk for 50 minutes to get home again.
I then microwave a meal for one, eat it, clean up after
myself and then I climb the stairs to fall into my bed,
completely fucked. I've always been a grafter though. I
can remember back when I was 19 and I got my first flat,
I was on the go 16 hours a day for weeks, just sorting the
place out. Transforming the home from a pensioner's
pad, to something more befitting a producer of Techno
records. Anyway, the flat was situated on a fairly
notorious estate on the outskirts of Belfast. Burning cars
in the street, gangs patrolling the area armed with
baseball bats, nightly domestic violence and joyriding.
My front door was kicked in, my windows were smashed
and every night the air was filled with the sound of the
screeching tyres of stolen cars, or the rumble of R.U.C.

jeeps. It was a proper shithole. You may be reading this blog in a similar set up. Hang in there. One afternoon I was shovelling coal into a bucket to fuel my fire for some hot water, and I suddenly thought "I'm going to live on a country estate in Scotland.". I'm not sure where that thought came from, and I never did anything at all to actively pursue that vision, but 10 years later I was living on a country estate in Scotland. Anyhow, the old bloke who had recently vacated the flat that I had moved into was now living above me in a larger apartment. I'd see him popping out for groceries, or he'd knock on my door to ask if any post had been delivered to my address for him, and each time he saw me I'd have a paintbrush, or a hammer in my hand. I'm not sure who he was shagging at the time, but it was so regular, and noisy, that I wrote a story about it. I printed about 100 copies of the story, and put them into food bags, along with some home made Techno on cassettes. I wrote "Free Techno" on each of the food bags, then I handed an armful of them into each of the independent music shops in Belfast city centre - there were loads of those shops back then, in the days before LimeWire. I even handed some personally to Terry

Hooley at his Good Vibrations shop. Terry was the man responsible for getting The Undertones record "Teenage Kicks" into the hands of John Peel. Well, the point of all of this gibberish is that I can quite clearly remember a couple of the things my old neighbour said to me. They were; "Do you ever just fucking chill out?" (For me, the answer to that question is always "No."), and "Whatever firm gets you are gonna be laughing. You never stop.". I'm not sure if the firm that did end up getting me have been laughing, but they've certainly had a trustworthy, capable and hard working man on their team for 12 years. This recent job has damaged me though. I ended up with chronic upper back pain. It went on for months. I was necking Ibuprofen, and Paracetamol and Codeine like they were Smarties, just to get through my working day. When my day's off finally rolled around, I'd spend the first of the two practically immovable, in agony. I was a mess. I had a fortnight's annual leave approaching though, at the end of July, and this, to me, was when I was going to make my remarkable recovery. Then, when I'd get back to work I'd be fit as a fiddle, and ready to crack on with things again, pain free. It didn't quite work out like that though. Not at all, in fact. Not at all.

At the start of my, em, "Holiday", I visited my doctor and explained my symptoms. By this stage in the game my upper back pain was so severe that I couldn't sit down. I was even carrying an empty backpack around, so that if people saw me walking funny, they'd just think I was weighed down by dismembered body parts, and not think twice about it. I mean, I do live in Leith after all. My doctor decided that the best course of action would be to refer me for an MRI scan, to see what was going on internally with my back. He also prescribed me a drug cocktail, which consisted of 30mg Paracetamol and Codeine tablets, Diazepam tranquillisers and the anti-inflammatory drug Naproxen. Now beyond this point, my memory of things begins to get a little fuzzy. That's due to the fact that the Naproxen I was taking had begun to make my stomach bleed. I was getting light headed, dizzy, short of breath, insomnia began to mess with my sense of time, and suddenly I was 1/3 of the man I once was, and I was still in pain. One night, a Tuesday I think, I was lying in bed feeling really weak, then all of a sudden I knew I was going to vomit. What followed was a period of 14 hours were I was throwing up, and shitting out, what looked like Guinness. Knowing that I hadn't spent the previous 3 days on a strict diet of squid ink, in between bouts of heaving I managed to alert one of my flatmates, a GP, to my plight. "What the fuck is this?" I enquired, both weakly, and eloquently. "I'm throwing up endless black stuff, and I haven't eaten anything black. It's been going on for hours.". My flatmate was able to tell me that I was passing blood, fresh blood. So, by early afternoon, and looking like a ghost I was back to see my doctor again. He changed my Paracetamol and Codeine to Tramadol and, more importantly, my Naproxen to Omeprazole. I gave a blood sample, then made my way, very, very, slowly home. Even whilst walking up slight inclines I was being overtaken by pensioners on their way to bingo halls, or wherever the Hell it is that they go to to buy light grey, or olive green clothing, before wearing it seven layers thick when the sun comes out. The sweat was pissing off me, my head was thumping, and I was drifting in and out of reality. Everything was hazy. It took a week to get my blood results, but I was asked to come in urgently at that point.

When I'm in my doctor's waiting room I stand at the window and lean against a pillar at the edge of the main area there until I hear my name being called. That way I get a view of Calton Hill, a light breeze, and I don't have to sit down which, as I've explained, is fucking agony. This time though, I was losing it, not in a dramatic, or angry way. What I mean is, I was losing consciousness. Thankfully my name was called and I stumbled in the direction of the female doctors voice. "Mr Clarke. Mr Clarke! You are very pale, and I have your results here. I'm going to have to ask you to go immediately to the hospital. Do you understand Mr Clarke?". She printed off a letter for me to hand in at the hospital. I had to ask the receptionist where I was going to, and how I could get there. "The Royal, son. Number 7 bus. It's very regular, just out on Great Junction Street there, on the opposite side of the road.". I think I nodded before I stumbled away, but I may have simply stumbled away, fuck knows.

Edinburgh buses don't give change, so I needed some coins to take me to Hell, or wherever it was I was headed to. I went into the wee shop they have at the surgery and asked for some change of a fiver from the elderly lady behind the till. I explained that I needed to go to hospital. "I think you do. Yes, defi-nate-ly, defi-nate-ly. I cannae open the till though, can't work it out at awl. Jesus, you look awful.". She then bought herself a packet of crisps for her lunch, and that opened the till, so I got my change - angel. I made my way to the bus stop and boarded the next available number 7 bus. I told the driver that I needed to go to the hospital, then made my way to the back of the bus and sat behind an old man. The sun was blinding me coming through the windows. I got a bit panicked when I realised all of my medication was at home. I mean, I'd just popped out to the doctors, I hadn't expected a bus ride to the hospital to suddenly become a part of my life. I text my mum and brother, possibly my flatmate. Then I tweeted about my latest release, "Renewable Energy", and promptly fell unconscious, resting my face against the back of the old man's head, as the bus trundled through Newington. Thankfully, the driver came and woke me up when we had reached the hospital. Otherwise, I'd have been on a bus, unconscious, doing circuits of Edinburgh deep into the night. By that point the old man, my pensioner pillow, had moved seats. I wonder how long it took him to move?

It took a while to walk from the bus stop to the A&E department. I was walking like a drunk most of the way, and far, far beyond the point of caring about it. Professional looking people were walking towards me at a brisk pace, whilst I stumbled and veered off course, and their conversations were circling my skull in a way that suggested I had perhaps put my head deep inside a wasps bike. The A&E waiting room, when I finally made it there, smelt strongly of weed. I gave the letter from my doctor to the girl behind the desk. I was then quickly whisked off to have a chest x-ray, for which I had to stand, in pain, trying not to faint as I held onto the handles at either side of the machine. After three failed attempts, and as I could feel my cold sweat crystallising on my back, they decided to change the battery in the x-ray machine - which was about the size of a car bonnet and required a two person lift. One zap later and I was suddenly in a room, well, behind a curtain, having an array of needles attached to me, including that one that stays in all the time at the bend in your arm like a fucking tap. I know I could Google the name of it, but it's rank enough just thinking about it, and you know the one I'm talking about anyway. After that, I was on my feet again, and staggering along behind the nurse who had just stabbed me. She took me a couple of curtains up the hall, to a dark room with a bed. Whoop! Result! Bedtime. I was knackered and on the bed with my eyes closed for what felt like 90 seconds, before I was woken up by a very attractive, young, brunette doctor, who was extraordinarily keen to slide one of her fingers deep inside my arse hole. Now, I'm sure for some of you filthy animals this sounds thrilling, and you're already working out how best to get some internal bleeding going on so you can get fingered by an attractive nurse for the mere price of a bus fair. Not me though, not this soldier. "Em, sorry. I'm nil by arse." I said. Because, seemingly, even when I'm completely out of it, I'm as sharp as a Stanley blade. She did her very best to persuade me otherwise, but it just wasn't going to be happening anytime this millennium. "Would you prefer a man to do it?", she enquired. "Erm, I don't think so. But, thank you for all of your kind offers so far." I said, dreading what the next response would be - "We have a team of lady boy's here at the hospital Mr Clarke. Perhaps that's more your thing?". I've since spoken to my GP flatmate about this, and she said it's relatively new that you can refuse an anal fingering down your local A&E department of an afternoon. I'm very glad I arrived in Hell relatively recently then, insomuch as my arse hole remaining un-fingered is a part of my daily routine, and has been for almost 37 years. I think I'm likely to die by arse. I think it'd be a fitting way for me to go. "Stephen? No! Jesus. How'd he die?". "Arse cancer.". "Ha, that's SO him!". After avoiding the lady finger, I was sat in a wheelchair in the middle of a corridor, where the lights were blinding my eyes. So, I just kind of collapsed, but I could still hear. I was used as an exhibit for a group of trainee hospital types. The doctor training them said, "This patient here is a classic case of their condition not matching their notes.". The students all agreed, and I was quickly wheeled away to the acute toxicology medical ward. On arrival, I was asked to take my shoes off and lie down on a bed. I wobbled my way out of the wheelchair, then swung by arse westerly as my arms flailed skyward. Perhaps this was a little unsightly, but I totally nailed the landing. Then the porter adjusted my bed so that I was nice and uncomfortable, before he disappeared, taking my favourite wheelchair with him. I was in Bed 1, obviously. I have a thing about me that just says "Bed 1". You've either got it, or you don't, and that afternoon you didn't have it, I did. I scanned the room for bodies. There were four beds in my section of the ward, and there was a nurses station in the middle of the unit. There was a wall directly behind the empty bed opposite mine - Bed 4, I presumed, and behind that I guessed there was another room similar to the one I was in. There must have been at least one bed in that room too, or perhaps a stable, as someone, or something, was snoring like a rutting deer. I looked to my left, Bed 2 was empty as well - lovely. There was a curtain pulled around Bed 3, which was in the corner diagonally opposite mine, next to the only window in the room. A couple of minutes later, after I'd spent a little time studying the tap in my arm and wishing I was dead, the curtain around Bed 3 was opened, in a rather violent fashion. I was then greeted by the site of a young, blonde, girl who was looking pretty rough (Mind you, I was looking pretty rough myself. Hospital is the very best place to be if you're looking rough though, no one minds at all. In fact, the rougher you look, the more attention you get. It's the polar opposite of the outside world.). The main difference between Bed 3, and my bed was that Bed 3 was being guarded by two Police Officers. While I remained a free man - free to collapse at least, my new blonde room mate seemed to be rather more restricted, option wise. Things were getting dark, and it wasn't even meal time yet. A nurse walked over and put one of those junkie arm bands around my left arm - the one that didn't have the tap in it, and started slapping my arm before informing me that "Yer veins are crap.". She then said, I might miss, before saying "Nah. Got it.". I was then given some cotton to hold against my new wound. I checked my phone - no signal, fuck. I then hid my wallet, since God knows what was going on in Bed 3, and then I promptly passed out.

I woke up to the sight of a nurse plugging my arm into a large, clear, drip. This was to be my one true companion for the next ten hours. The good news was that Bed 3 was now vacant, so I had the room to myself. I could smell food, it must be dinner time. I didn't feel particularly hungry, but that wasn't going to be a problem for long. As the male nurse/tea boy, whatever he was, minced passed the end of my bed he shouted, "That's everyone fed who's conscious, apart from Bed 1.". Then he swiped his fob against a sensor, a door opened and he disappeared through it, never to be seen again. I soon found out from a passing nurse that I was "Nil by mouth". Peachy. I was in pain, so I explained to the nurse that my drugs were at home, and she said not to worry. She'd look it up on their system and get some for me, "Oh, and by the way, your Mum has phoned LOTS while you were sleeping.". I explained to her that I had no signal on my phone, and she pointed to one at the nurses station. "Press 9 for an outside line love.". Then she darted off to get my dope for the evening - angel. I've never been attached to a drip before, never mind having to drag one across a ward with a low level of blood in my system, all the while trying to remember the dialling code for Belfast. However, I made it to the phone, a little faint, but proud of myself. I picked up the receiver, dialled the number and got the front desk. I hung up, pressed 9 and dialled the number once more. I can't remember what I talked to my Mum about, but I'm sure it wasn't much. I'm crap on the phone anyway, never mind when I'm stood in the middle of a ward, feeling faint, attached to a drip, with a group of five nurses looking at me. I finished my call, then realised I was busting for a piss, so I made my way to the loo. "Hi, sorry to bother you, but there's no lock on the toilet door.". "That's right sir, it's in case you faint.". "Oh, O.K.". So I stood there, in the loo, attached to a drip, taking a piss that seemed to last longer than a bank holiday weekend, in a ward where the only locked doors were the main entrance doors, and the door to the room where the drugs were kept. Why though? It was so quiet here, just me and the rutting stag and the ringing phone. I washed my hands, dried them and opened the door. A nurse greeted me with, "That's your Mum on the phone, AGAIN.". "Jesus, I'm sorry. I really do apologise.". "Just tell her it's lights out on the ward." and she winked at me - angel. After I'd delivered the word perfect lie to my Mother, provided to me for free, at no extra cost, by our wonderful NHS, it was time for bed again. I got myself into a position where I felt least likely to rip out my drip in the night, took my drugs and fell asleep.

I was woken up, rather abruptly, after only an hour's sleep, by an elderly lady sitting on the edge of my bed. She wasn't only on the edge of my bed though, she was on the edge in general. "I'm in Gorgie and there are two frogs. If my father was here! Shite! Pigs! If my husband was here. He's dead. You're all drunk!", she said, screamed and yelled in several different voices. Ah, so THIS is why the doors are locked, I thought. That line from the film Taxi Driver drifted though my weary head; "All the animals come out at night.". I had just done some training at work relating to people with dementia, so I honed in on the word Gorgie. "I used to live in Gorgie you know. Stafford Street. Apparently, where the new build apartments are now there used to be a great factory, who treated their staff very well, and were well known for throwing fantastic Christmas parties." I said, rather excitedly - being so fucking delighted that I'd never, ever, sleep again. Her face was blank. Eventually she barked the word "Haymarket!" at me, and then went off to search for crisps in a yellow sharps bin at the nurses station. Ordinarily, I'd have been dashing across to save her, but seeing as I had little blood, and even less sleep in me, I just sat back and watched the drama unfold. It went on for hours, all the while there were little old ladies doing laps of the nurses station, or sliding along the walls. Some huge guy was in the toilet at the far side of the ward. He was shouting about how he was full of shit, "But, the fucker isn't budging!". Meanwhile Little Miss Haymarket was becoming more and more deranged and nasty. She was pulling phones out of walls, throwing her slippers at the nurses. Her violence soon escalated, and she headbutted the young nurse who had been so helpful to me, regarding my need to throw the fucking phone in the bin when my Mum phoned twice in a row. Haymarket then began scratching and biting every member of staff she could get her hands on, before she was tackled onto a bed and given a shot in the arm. Personally, I'd have rammed the fucking needle into her eyeball, but I'm old fashioned like that. The injection in the arm is more up to scratch with modern training techniques. A consultant had been dragged from his bed to oversee the tranquillising, and he commented that he'd never seen anything like it, "Normally they're like a broken record, but this one is fascinating. She's visiting many different parts of her brain.". Shortly after that madness died down, and Haymarket was removed from my part of the ward, all Hell broke loose again. A man was brought into the room making wild sounds, the like of which I'd never heard before. Think Tarzan with constipation straining on the loo, then fire in a weeping choir of schoolboys and a baboon playing with a basketball and you'll be getting close the sounds I endured that night. This daft prick was put into Bed 2, right beside me. He'd spent the evening filling himself up with 15 Valium tablets, and an unknown quantity of Heroin. He had puncture wounds all over his body, and he was put on a drip that was smaller than mine, and looked like it was filled with a dehydrated person's piss. Bed 3 then received a suspected Meningitis case. The sound effects were similar in nature to that of the guy in Bed 2, but this time they were emanating from a woman. Shortly after that a young girl arrived to take up residency in Bed 4. She was there because she had taken an overdose of her Mum's pills. All the while, the little old ladies did laps of the nurses station, or slid backwards along the wall. It was a nightmare, but somehow, at some point, I fell asleep.

I woke up, well, actually I didn't fully wake up, as a nurse checked my blood pressure. She even put a strap around my wrist and took blood from my hand without me caring too much about it. I think I was just so exhausted, and so ill that I barely felt like I was there. Not long after that the curtains were pulled around my bed, and a beautiful blonde, Scandinavian, lady asked me questions about how I was feeling. Then she told me that I was borderline for a blood transfusion, but that my blood had improved by one point since the test at my doctors surgery, so they had decided not to do it. I could repair myself, which was the better option. Although this process would take around three months. "You are booked in for a scope between 2 and 3 o'clock today Mr Clarke. I've noticed that we have yet to examine your back passage. Would it be possible for me to do that?". "No. No, not today. Thank you though.". "Would you prefer a man?". "No, I would not. I'm nil by arse.". She then removed my drip. I felt like shit. I hadn't eaten in 26 hours, and I needed to piss again. At least that killed twenty minutes or so, while I waited for my visit to Scope Land. I began humming that old Michael Jackson song; "Heal the gut. Make it a better gut...". By the time I came out of the pisser all the crazy old people had left. Beamed back up to the mother-ship, or wherever they came from. The parents of the young overdose patient visited, briefly. They both had a look on their face that said "Again?". They looked burnt out. Everyone in the room looked burnt out, apart from the junkie in Bed 2 who kept shouting for drugs, but no one came to his aid, and I really enjoyed that. Cheered me right up. Prick. Shortly after that I was moved away from the Toxicology ward, and placed in a General ward, to await my scope. I was the youngest person in the room by a long, long way. This was coffin dodger city. Even the nurses in this ward looked like patients. It wasn't too long before I was lying down on a mobile bed, ready to go. I told the porter I was going to get a scope, and an old guy in the bed next to me said, "They'll tell you it tastes like bananas. It doesn't.". And, with that, I was off, racing towards Scope World Of Adventure. When I arrived, a helpful assistant gave me the low-down; I could get drugged up, or have a simple throat spray. If I went the throat spray route, provided I got the all clear, I could leave tonight. "I'll have the spray please." I said, confidently.

The scope itself wasn't too awful. I mean, I wouldn't take a ticket off your hands for a free one, but if my stomach explodes again, I'd be OK with another run through. Basically they spray your throat and then they lie to you about how nice and easy the whole procedure is going to be. You're then rolled over onto your side before they put a plastic circle thing your mouth, so that you can't close it, or bite down, and you look like a blow up sex doll. Then they feed the tube through your mouth, and the whole way down into your stomach. Slow and steady breathing is the key to stopping the gag reflex, but I still gagged from time to time, as my eyes watered and winced. They blow air into you as well, to open up the valves and tubes and whatever the fuck your insides are made of, in order that they can shove the camera in deeper. This makes you burp, which was obviously a lot of fun, for nobody. Then they take some holiday snapshots inside you. Mine featured a series of ulcers that were healing, but they were able to do a bit of work on them while they were in there as well. Then they remove the camera, and your chest and throat are sore for a couple of days afterwards. I was supposed to be able to watch the screen while they were doing it, which would have been kind of cool, but it was being viewed by the students that I'd agreed could watch my ordeal. So, instead, I just got a view of the crotch of the Scandinavian lady who had interviewed me earlier in the day and had asked me if she could finger my arse hole. At some point during the procedure I did start thinking;

"Is this camera going to come out of my butt? Is this her revenge?". However, I can confirm that my arse remained untouched throughout. Although, I did have another lady rubbing my head and neck, and wiping my sweat and tears away throughout. I think she just came in off the street to help out, you know, since it was me - angel. The throat spray tastes like bananas, in the same way that shoe polish tastes like an apple.

I was soon back on the ward of the nearly dead, and I couldn't wait to get out of there. There was an old guy pissing into a bottle and all over the bed to the left of me, and to the right there was an old lady, whom I was sure had died months ago and just been left there due to a clerical error. Anyway, dead or not, she managed to shit herself just as dinner was being served. Thankfully my scope results showed that my ulcers were healing, but there was a pool of blood in my stomach that was still to come out. The nurse in charge of Death Row wanted to keep me in overnight, but thankfully it wasn't up to her. I noticed a female doctor looking through my notes and I did my best to look sparkling. Now, I'm pretty sure I looked awful, because I still do, but compared to the living dead who were strewn all around me, I was looking good. I sat up on the edge of my bed, put my shoes on (cheeky), and used my Irish charm to good effect. She authorised my discharge! This pissed off the main ward nurse, who insisted I eat a full hospital meal, with the smell of old lady shit filling my nostrils, and with my throat, and the whole tube, or whatever it's called, to my stomach on fire. This didn't phase me slightly. Get in my way and I'll go through you for a shortcut, every time - Them's the rules kid. So, I scoffed the lot in no time, horrible as it was. Then I stood up, put my coat on and waited at her desk for her to sign me out. Which she did, eventually. You know, after cleaning up old lady shit.

I was home, in my own bed, by about 8pm and it was lush. Somehow, my single tweet about my new release, "Renewable Energy", had managed to drum up some sales in the USA, Germany, Italy, Belgium, Holland and the UK, and I was asked to write a blog about the return of The KLF, which I did, from my sick bed - it was hugely successful. Then I was featured in the line up for The Dark Outside 2017, alongside the likes of Depeche Mode, Delia Derbyshire, Laurie Anderson, Scanner, The Black Dog and Tom Middleton. Frankly, that's a life highlight for me. At the minute, health wise, I'm still recovering. I've got another doctors appointment today, to go over the results of an MRI scan, and to have my bloods checked. I'm having a think about where my future lies, and whilst I'm in my current state, I just can't see it being in a manual job. In fact, just now at least, I'm doing pretty well just working from my bed.

ON DELETED SCENES

06.10.2017

When I wrote the story "Fried Chicken", back in November of last year, I knew that it was going to be the first chapter of my autobiography. Even though prior to penning it I can't ever remember writing anything other than lyrics and poetry, the concept of writing a whole book didn't seem daunting. However, during my years running Edinburgh Dream Factory I did send out the occasional lengthy e-mail to my followers, usually mocking the very scene I was part of, in an attempt to wake them up and make them think. These outbursts did cause a bit of a stir at times, which I quite enjoyed. The reactions varied from "I think you're onto something here." to "Please remove me from your mailing list.". Some things change, and some things don't. A decade later and I'm still more than happy to question the things that most people take for granted. I was born a rebel, and I grew up very street wise during The Troubles in Northern Ireland. I think fast, go with my instincts and take action. So, when this idea of writing a book came into my head, I just saw it as another job that needed doing. In the end it has taken me less than a year to write, and it was completed whilst I was working in a full time job that was so physically draining that, at times, I was only managing to write one chapter a month. I never stopped though. All progress is still progress.

As far as the subject matter goes, I tried my best to stick to a ten year rule. That rule meant not writing in any great detail about the many major events that have happened in my life over the past decade. If I'm still around in another ten years, perhaps those stories will surface then. I think it takes around a decade before an event becomes a story anyway. Real life is confusing and messy in the moment, but as time passes our minds seem to naturally find a simple, linear, narrative that conveniently trims and polishes our past into nice, easy to understand, tales. Some names and places have been changed to protect both the innocent and the guilty, and in each of the recollections that I explore you are very much exposed to my telling of the story, it is my book after all. Over the past few days I have read all of the chapters of this book, whilst making the occasional edit and pondering if I should change the running order about, in an attempt to give the whole project more of a start, middle and end. However, after mulling it over, I have decided to just publish the stories in the sequence in which they were written.

The title, "Deleted Scenes", grew out of the way that I tend to delete online posts, and begin anew. I also throw out my wardrobe every once in a while, and buy some more items that suit the new me. I'm afraid I have also done this with human beings as well. Sometimes I'll have a look through my old shoe box full of photographs taken in my earlier years, before my life switched from analogue to digital; Every picture in there is of a deleted scene. I'm just very much drawn to new starts. I love how all over the place The Beatles, or The KLF's back catalogues are; Trying different sounds, looks and ideas – even working under different aliases (Sgt. Pepper's Lonely Hearts Club Band / The Justified Ancients Of Mu Mu). When it comes to my work, I'm very much focused on the present and totally prepared to burn any bridge to the past at any given moment, with no regrets whatsoever.

When I was 14 years old I made a work of art for my aunt, Michelle, who shares her birthday with me (Well, I arrived 14 years after her and gatecrashed her birthday really, and I've been doing so annually ever since). The art work, titled "Ready For Something", consisted of a blank white A4 sheet of office paper, with another, smaller sheet of slightly fancier plain white paper, with torn edges, glued to the middle of the office paper. The whole construction was mounted, then placed inside a plain, black, frame. It looked pretty cool, and it made you think. In fact Michelle wrote to me recently mentioning the piece, therefore the idea has resonated with her for 23 years. So, I guess the whole idea of fresh starts has been a big driving factor inside me for a long time. With each new beginning I feel like I get another shot at gaining my own footnote in the appendix of the "New Illustrated Rock Handbook", or whatever it's modern equivalent is. Stranger things have happened.

I got the results of my MRI scan, and they weren't good. It's been recommended that I have surgery on two separate parts of my spine. I'm still anemic, and I'm currently taking 31 pills a day for my various health problems. I may be at a rather low point in my life physically, but creatively things are really going well, and I'm feeling positive that, slowly at least, I can begin to start paying my way in life with the profits from my creative adventures, rather than the money I make from stacking shelves. If that doesn't quite work out, I can always delete this book and start again.

Keep dreaming.

Stephen Clarke 1980

POST SCRIPT;

It's around 4:30pm and my postman has just been and gone, much later than usual. He told me that it's been a bad day, and everything has been held up. I tried to lighten the mood by saying "Oh well, at least it's Friday.". I think that helped, as he stopped complaining and just handed me a rather large collection of parcels, and a single letter. "This one needs signed for.", he said. "No worries." I replied, as I squiggled my signature onto his digital keypad with my index finger. He closed the front door for me, and I made my way upstairs laden with parcels to open on the kitchen table. There were a set of black plastic shelves that I had ordered, to use as a bookcase for my ever growing collection of autobiographies and books about music, photography and art. A Steve Coogan box set had also arrived. It includes both series of Saxondale – my favourite of his characters (As an aside, my uncle once bought a flat in London from Steve Coogan. So, I can confirm that I've pissed in the same pot as Alan Partridge.). A black T-shirt had also been delivered for me, with a picture of a disgruntled Tommy Saxondale on the front, and the words "Yada.. Yada.. Yada." written underneath his bearded face. I lay the T-shirt down on the table and opened the single letter that I'd signed for. It was a "Form SP16 – Extract Decree of Divorce", from Perth Sheriff Court and Justice of the Peace Court. I placed my Decree of Divorce on top of my new T-shirt, just below the words "Yada.. Yada.. Yada.", before I took in the scene for a moment. I couldn't think of anyone better to be there with me when I opened that letter than Tommy Saxondale, and I also can't think of anything better to say about it all at this time, other than "Yada.. Yada.. Yada.".

THE END.

STEPHEN CLARKE 1980

Northern Irish writer, electronic musician and visual artist.

https://stephenclarke1980.bandcamp.com/

https://twitter.com/stephenclarke80

https://stephenclarke1980.wordpress.com/

https://soundcloud.com/stephenclarke1980

https://www.youtube.com/channel/UCVMKy7LZVxpAJMJ

OIJYXwsQ

25202851R00103

Printed in Great Britain
by Amazon